The Library of Congress /

027.573 Sim

Simpson, Andrew L.

162763

DATE

ISSUED TO

The Library of Congress

KNOW YOUR GOVERNMENT

The Library of Congress

Andrew L. Simpson

CHELSEA HOUSE PUBLISHERS

Chelsea House Publishers
Editor-in-Chief: Nancy Toff
Executive Editor: Remmel T. Nunn
Managing Editor: Karyn Gullen Browne
Copy Chief: Juliann Barbato
Picture Editor: Adrian G. Allen
Art Director: Maria Epes
Manufacturing Manager: Gerald Levine

Know Your Government
Senior Editor: Kathy Kuhtz

Staff for THE LIBRARY OF CONGRESS
Assistant Editor: Karen Schimmel
Copy Editor: Nicole Bowen
Deputy Copy Chief: Ellen Scordato
Editorial Assistant: Elizabeth Nix
Picture Coordinator: Michèle Brisson
Picture Researcher: Dixon and Turner Research Associates, Inc.
Assistant Art Director: Loraine Machlin
Senior Designer: Noreen M. Lamb
Layout: Arlene Goldberg
Production Coordinator: Joseph Romano

First Printing

1 3 5 7 9 8 6 4 2

Library of Congress Cataloging-in-Publication Data
Simpson, Andrew L.
   The Library of Congress.
   (Know your government)
   Bibliography: p.
   Summary: Surveys the history of the Library of Congress and describes its structure, functions, and influence on United States society.
   1. Library of Congress. 2. Libraries, National—United States—History. 3. Libraries, Governmental, administrative, etc.—United States—History.
[1. Library of Congress.   2. Libraries]   I. Title.
II. Series: Know your government (New York, N.Y.)
Z733.U6H34   1989   027.573   88-34014
ISBN 1-55546-109-3
       0-7910-0900-0 (pbk.)

CONTENTS

KNOW YOUR GOVERNMENT

CHELSEA HOUSE PUBLISHERS

INTRODUCTION

Government: Crises of Confidence

Arthur M. Schlesinger, jr.

From the start, Americans have regarded their government with a mixture of reliance and mistrust. The men who founded the republic did not doubt the indispensability of government. "If men were angels," observed the 51st Federalist Paper, "no government would be necessary." But men are not angels. Because human beings are subject to wicked as well as to noble impulses, government was deemed essential to assure freedom and order.

At the same time, the American revolutionaries knew that government could also become a source of injury and oppression. The men who gathered in Philadelphia in 1787 to write the Constitution therefore had two purposes in mind. They wanted to establish a strong central authority and to limit that central authority's capacity to abuse its power.

To prevent the abuse of power, the Founding Fathers wrote two basic principles into the new Constitution. The principle of federalism divided power between the state governments and the central authority. The principle of the separation of powers subdivided the central authority itself into three branches—the executive, the legislative, and the judiciary—so that "each may be a check on the other." The *Know Your Government* series focuses on the major executive departments and agencies in these branches of the federal government.

7

The Constitution did not plan the executive branch in any detail. After vesting the executive power in the president, it assumed the existence of "executive departments" without specifying what these departments should be. Congress began defining their functions in 1789 by creating the Departments of State, Treasury, and War. The secretaries in charge of these departments made up President Washington's first cabinet. Congress also provided for a legal officer, and President Washington soon invited the attorney general, as he was called, to attend cabinet meetings. As need required, Congress created more executive departments.

Setting up the cabinet was only the first step in organizing the American state. With almost no guidance from the Constitution, President Washington, seconded by Alexander Hamilton, his brilliant secretary of the treasury, equipped the infant republic with a working administrative structure. The Federalists believed in both executive energy and executive accountability and set high standards for public appointments. The Jeffersonian opposition had less faith in strong government and preferred local government to the central authority. But when Jefferson himself became president in 1801, although he set out to change the direction of policy, he found no reason to alter the framework the Federalists had erected.

By 1801 there were about 3,000 federal civilian employees in a nation of a little more than 5 million people. Growth in territory and population steadily enlarged national responsibilities. Thirty years later, when Jackson was president, there were more than 11,000 government workers in a nation of 13 million. The federal establishment was increasing at a faster rate than the population.

Jackson's presidency brought significant changes in the federal service. He believed that the executive branch contained too many officials who saw their jobs as "species of property" and as "a means of promoting individual interest." Against the idea of a permanent service based on life tenure, Jackson argued for the periodic redistribution of federal offices, contending that this was the democratic way and that official duties could be made "so plain and simple that men of intelligence may readily qualify themselves for their performance." He called this policy rotation-in-office. His opponents called it the spoils system.

In fact, partisan legend exaggerated the extent of Jackson's removals. More than 80 percent of federal officeholders retained their jobs. Jackson discharged no larger a proportion of government workers than Jefferson had done a generation earlier. But the rise in these years of mass political parties gave federal patronage new importance as a means of building the party and of rewarding activists. Jackson's successors were less restrained in the distribu-

8

tion of spoils. As the federal establishment grew—to nearly 40,000 by 1861—the politicization of the public service excited increasing concern.

After the Civil War the spoils system became a major political issue. High-minded men condemned it as the root of all political evil. The spoilsmen, said the British commentator James Bryce, "have distorted and depraved the mechanism of politics." Patronage, by giving jobs to unqualified, incompetent, and dishonest persons, lowered the standards of public service and nourished corrupt political machines. Office-seekers pursued presidents and cabinet secretaries without mercy. "Patronage," said Ulysses S. Grant after his presidency, "is the bane of the presidential office." "Every time I appoint someone to office," said another political leader, "I make a hundred enemies and one ingrate." George William Curtis, the president of the National Civil Service Reform League, summed up the indictment. He said,

> The theory which perverts public trusts into party spoils, making public
> employment dependent upon personal favor and not on proved merit,
> necessarily ruins the self-respect of public employees, destroys the
> function of party in a republic, prostitutes elections into a desperate
> strife for personal profit, and degrades the national character by lower-
> ing the moral tone and standard of the country.

The object of civil service reform was to promote efficiency and honesty in the public service and to bring about the ethical regeneration of public life. Over bitter opposition from politicians, the reformers in 1883 passed the Pendleton Act, establishing a bipartisan Civil Service Commission, competitive examinations, and appointment on merit. The Pendleton Act also gave the president authority to extend by executive order the number of "classified" jobs—that is, jobs subject to the merit system. The act applied initially only to about 14,000 of the more than 100,000 federal positions. But by the end of the 19th century 40 percent of federal jobs had moved into the classified category.

Civil service reform was in part a response to the growing complexity of American life. As society grew more organized and problems more technical, official duties were no longer so plain and simple that any person of intelligence could perform them. In public service, as in other areas, the all-round man was yielding ground to the expert, the amateur to the professional. The excesses of the spoils system thus provoked the counter-ideal of scientific public administration, separate from politics and, as far as possible, insulated against it.

The cult of the expert, however, had its own excesses. The idea that administration could be divorced from policy was an illusion. And in the realm of policy, the expert, however much segregated from partisan politics, can never attain perfect objectivity. He remains the prisoner of his own set of values. It is these values rather than technical expertise that determine fundamental judgments of public policy. To turn over such judgments to experts, moreover, would be to abandon democracy itself; for in a democracy final decisions must be made by the people and their elected representatives. "The business of the expert," the British political scientist Harold Laski rightly said, "is to be on tap and not on top."

Politics, however, were deeply ingrained in American folkways. This meant intermittent tension between the presidential government, elected every four years by the people, and the permanent government, which saw presidents come and go while it went on forever. Sometimes the permanent government knew better than its political masters; sometimes it opposed or sabotaged valuable new initiatives. In the end a strong president with effective cabinet secretaries could make the permanent government responsive to presidential purpose, but it was often an exasperating struggle.

The struggle within the executive branch was less important, however, than the growing impatience with bureaucracy in society as a whole. The 20th century saw a considerable expansion of the federal establishment. The Great Depression and the New Deal led the national government to take on a variety of new responsibilities. The New Deal extended the federal regulatory apparatus. By 1940, in a nation of 130 million people, the number of federal workers for the first time passed the 1 million mark. The Second World War brought federal civilian employment to 3.8 million in 1945. With peace, the federal establishment declined to around 2 million by 1950. Then growth resumed, reaching 2.8 million by the 1980s.

The New Deal years saw rising criticism of "big government" and "bureaucracy." Businessmen resented federal regulation. Conservatives worried about the impact of paternalistic government on individual self-reliance, on community responsibility, and on economic and personal freedom. The nation in effect renewed the old debate between Hamilton and Jefferson in the early republic, although with an ironic exchange of positions. For the Hamiltonian constituency, the "rich and well-born," once the advocate of affirmative government, now condemned government intervention, while the Jeffersonian constituency, the plain people, once the advocate of a weak central government and of states' rights, now favored government intervention.

In the 1980s, with the presidency of Ronald Reagan, the debate has burst out with unusual intensity. According to conservatives, government intervention abridges liberty, stifles enterprise, and is inefficient, wasteful, and arbitrary. It disturbs the harmony of the self-adjusting market and creates worse troubles than it solves. Get government off our backs, according to the popular cliché, and our problems will solve themselves. When government is necessary, let it be at the local level, close to the people. Above all, stop the inexorable growth of the federal government.

In fact, for all the talk about the "swollen" and "bloated" bureaucracy, the federal establishment has not been growing as inexorably as many Americans seem to believe. In 1949, it consisted of 2.1 million people. Thirty years later, while the country had grown by 70 million, the federal force had grown only by 750,000. Federal workers were a smaller percentage of the population in 1985 than they were in 1955—or in 1940. The federal establishment, in short, has not kept pace with population growth. Moreover, national defense and the postal service account for 60 percent of federal employment.

Why then the widespread idea about the remorseless growth of government? It is partly because in the 1960s the national government assumed new and intrusive functions: affirmative action in civil rights, environmental protection, safety and health in the workplace, community organization, legal aid to the poor. Although this enlargement of the federal regulatory role was accompanied by marked growth in the size of government on all levels, the expansion has taken place primarily in state and local government. Whereas the federal force increased by only 27 percent in the 30 years after 1950, the state and local government force increased by an astonishing 212 percent.

Despite the statistics, the conviction flourishes in some minds that the national government is a steadily growing behemoth swallowing up the liberties of the people. The foes of Washington prefer local government, feeling it is closer to the people and therefore allegedly more responsive to popular needs. Obviously there is a great deal to be said for settling local questions locally. But local government is characteristically the government of the locally powerful. Historically, the way the locally powerless have won their human and constitutional rights has often been through appeal to the national government. The national government has vindicated racial justice against local bigotry, defended the Bill of Rights against local vigilantism, and protected natural resources against local greed. It has civilized industry and secured the rights of labor organizations. Had the states' rights creed prevailed, there would perhaps still be slavery in the United States.

The national authority, far from diminishing the individual, has given most Americans more personal dignity and liberty than ever before. The individual freedoms destroyed by the increase in national authority have been in the main the freedom to deny black Americans their rights as citizens; the freedom to put small children to work in mills and immigrants in sweatshops; the freedom to pay starvation wages, require barbarous working hours, and permit squalid working conditions; the freedom to deceive in the sale of goods and securities; the freedom to pollute the environment—all freedoms that, one supposes, a civilized nation can readily do without.

"Statements are made," said President John F. Kennedy in 1963, "labelling the Federal Government an outsider, an intruder, an adversary. . . . The United States Government is not a stranger or not an enemy. It is the people of fifty states joining in a national effort. . . . Only a great national effort by a great people working together can explore the mysteries of space, harvest the products at the bottom of the ocean, and mobilize the human, natural, and material resources of our lands."

So an old debate continues. However, Americans are of two minds. When pollsters ask large, spacious questions—Do you think government has become too involved in your lives? Do you think government should stop regulating business?—a sizable majority opposes big government. But when asked specific questions about the practical work of government—Do you favor social security? unemployment compensation? Medicare? health and safety standards in factories? environmental protection? government guarantee of jobs for everyone seeking employment? price and wage controls when inflation threatens?—a sizable majority approves of intervention.

In general, Americans do not want less government. What they want is more efficient government. They want government to do a better job. For a time in the 1970s, with Vietnam and Watergate, Americans lost confidence in the national government. In 1964, more than three-quarters of those polled had thought the national government could be trusted to do right most of the time. By 1980 only one-quarter was prepared to offer such trust. But by 1984 trust in the federal government to manage national affairs had climbed back to 45 percent.

Bureaucracy is a term of abuse. But it is impossible to run any large organization, whether public or private, without a bureaucracy's division of labor and hierarchy of authority. And we live in a world of large organizations. Without bureaucracy modern society would collapse. The problem is not to abolish bureaucracy, but to make it flexible, efficient, and capable of innovation.

Two hundred years after the drafting of the Constitution, Americans still regard government with a mixture of reliance and mistrust—a good combination. Mistrust is the best way to keep government reliable. Informed criticism is the means of correcting governmental inefficiency, incompetence, and arbitrariness; that is, of best enabling government to play its essential role. For without government, we cannot attain the goals of the Founding Fathers. Without an understanding of government, we cannot have the informed criticism that makes government do the job right. It is the duty of every American citizen to know our government—which is what this series is all about.

The Great Hall of the Library of Congress in Washington, D.C. Completed in 1897, the new Library was designed in the architectural style of the Italian Renaissance to symbolize America's earnest commitment to a great age of learning.

ONE

The Nation's Library

Since ancient times, libraries, or collections of books, have been valued for the information they contain. Long before the English philosopher Francis Bacon (1561–1626) wrote that "Knowledge itself is power," libraries were jealously guarded fortresses of information, access to which enabled the possessors to exert control over large numbers of people. In their earliest form, libraries were archives or holdings of official papers—rooms adjacent to palaces or temples that contained state records and religious secrets. Their growth paralleled the rise of great civilizations, of man's striving for knowledge of himself and of the universe.

Throughout most of human history, libraries have been accessible to very few—to rulers, nobles, priests, and their scribes. The pleasures of learning, and of book collecting, have been celebrated since ancient times, but until the 18th century these pursuits were enjoyed only by those sufficiently wealthy and powerful to afford such luxuries and to be permitted them. The common people generally did not read and write, for lack of time and opportunity or by the design of their rulers. Not surprisingly, most of the great libraries of the world today, such as the Bibliothèque Nationale of France, originated as royal or princely collections or were effectively controlled by the will of monarchs.

15

The Bibliotèque Nationale, in Paris, France, like many great librar-
ies of the world, originated as a royal book collection, accessible only
to the wealthy. The Library of Congress, on the other hand, began as
a collection of reference books for members of Congress to use while
drafting legislation.

The Library of Congress has had a much different history. It began in the
early years of American independence as a small collection of reference books
that members of Congress consulted in drafting legislation and overseeing the
new nation's foreign affairs. Congress's library grew gradually and emerged as
an important national and international institution soon after the United States
rose to a position of world power in the late 19th century. Today it is the
largest library in the world.

Three principal buildings adjacent to the U.S. Capitol house the collections
of the Library of Congress, which in 1988 consisted of more than 85 million
items. Its holdings include more than 20 million books and pamphlets, 36 million

manuscripts, 4 million maps and atlases, 10 million prints and photographs, and 3 million musical works. In addition the Library contains about 6 million microforms—for example, microfiche and flat transparencies—500,000 sound recordings, and almost that same number of motion picture reels. Its computer system holds 12.5 million records in its data bases. The Library employs about 5,000 individuals to maintain and interpret these vast holdings for the benefit of Congress, other libraries throughout the world, and the public.

Throughout its history the Library of Congress has remained Congress's library, loaning books and other materials to members of the Senate and House of Representatives and their staffs. Through two of its major departments, the Congressional Research Service and the Law Library, it provides direct research support to Congress. The Congressional Research Service handles requests for information of all kinds made by members of Congress (in 1987 alone these amounted to 443,433 inquiries). The Law Library loans materials to and responds to queries from Congress and other federal agencies on questions pertaining to the laws of the United States and those of foreign nations (in 1986 it handled more than 670,000 inquiries).

The Library of Congress is also the national library of the United States. It was opened to the public as early as the 1830s and remains today the least restrictive of the major national libraries in the world. Readers 18 years of age or older are permitted to use the general collections; access to the rare and special collections is based upon the purpose of the research or the investigation the reader is undertaking. The Library of Congress facilitates research throughout the country by producing a wide variety of bibliographical services and publications, performing photoduplication services, supervising and coordinating purchases of foreign books and materials, making interlibrary loans, and maintaining a network for the production and loan of reading materials to the blind and physically handicapped.

In the late 20th century the Library of Congress has increasingly become a national information center. It has made use of modern computer technologies to automate its vast catalog of holdings and to transfer deteriorating paper materials to new media that offer alternative solutions for storage and library services. It has positioned itself to become a "multimedia encyclopedia" for the Congress and the nation in this new age that is shaped by the flow of information.

At the same time, the Library continues to grow in importance as a national cultural center. Through concerts, exhibitions, readings of poetry, lectures, and publications, the Library interprets and preserves the cultural heritage of language in American—and world—civilization. It has become a center for the

The Thomas Jefferson Building, one of three principal buildings housing the collections of the Library of Congress, is located across from the U.S. Capitol. Among the Library divisions found here are the American Folklife Center, the Rare Book and Special Collections Division, the Local History and Genealogy Reading Room, and the Computer Catalog Center.

study and appreciation of the printed word and the promotion of reading in national life.

Through the elected members of Congress the Library of Congress has reflected the values and aspirations of the American people. In the 20th century this great national institution has substantially influenced the nation's perceptions of itself and of the world. It will continue to be influential as long as America values its democratic institutions and the American electorate values knowledge, for, in the words of the Library's greatest historical figure, Librarian Ainsworth Rand Spofford, the United States is "a Republic which rests upon the popular intelligence."

President Thomas Jefferson was instrumental in setting up the first Library of Congress; he assisted the Joint Committee on the Library in selecting titles and appointed John James Beckley as the first librarian of Congress.

TWO

Early History: The Congressional Library, 1800–1897

W hen members of the Continental Congress voted to proclaim independence from Great Britain in 1776, they set out on a new and largely uncharted course. They cast off the colonial government of Great Britain and its king, George III, and formed the first truly representative republic in modern times. "We, the People," the first words of the new Constitution—which was signed in 1787 and ratified two years later—made it clear from where the authority of the new government in America derived.

The grand words of the Declaration of Independence and the U.S. Constitution are inscribed in marble today, but at the time they were written the success of America's "republican experiment" was not at all certain. American lawmakers were very much aware that most attempts at a representative government in any age had failed: The ambitions and hopes of the people had invariably ended in the despotism of a single ruler or small group of rulers. The framers of the U.S. Constitution did not want history to repeat itself. To guard against the mistakes of the past, they determined to let history be their guide in setting up and administering the new federal government.

America's lawmakers wanted to know as much as they could about the experiences of other nations, ancient and modern. When Congress first met in New York and later in Philadelphia, members were able to borrow and consult important editions on history, economics, and government from local library companies or clubs. The new capital, Washington, however, was only a small village when the federal government moved there in 1800, and it had no such collections. A library for Congress therefore became a necessity. Anticipating this need, William Thornton had included a library to occupy a room of importance in his architectural plans for the new U.S. Capitol, which were approved in 1793. Although the first members of Congress disagreed on particular issues, they could all agree with Virginia senator John Randolph, who believed that a good library was "a statesman's workshop."

As the Senate and the House of Representatives prepared to move into the newly completed north wing of the Capitol in 1800, Congress appropriated $5,000 to purchase books and place them in "one suitable apartment" in the Capitol for the use of members of both houses, thus establishing the Library of Congress. The 152 titles, selected by a joint committee of both houses, included works on British law and parliamentary history, histories of ancient and modern Europe, geographies and travel accounts, legal treatises and

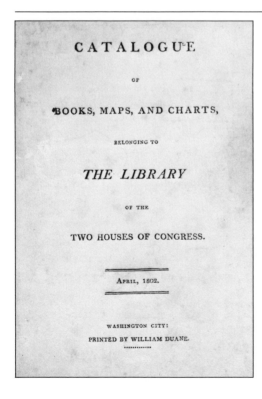

The Library's first catalog of its holdings, published in 1802, consisted of 152 items.

studies of international law, and works on trade and commerce. Such was the state of publishing in the new nation that this first order for the new library had to be placed with a bookseller in England. These books and several maps arrived safely by ship from London in 11 trunks early in 1801.

Almost a year later, on January 26, 1802, Congress passed the first "Act Concerning the Library for the Use of Both Houses of Congress." This law provided for a librarian to be appointed by the president of the United States. The librarian of Congress would be paid "a sum not exceeding two dollars . . . for every day of necessary attendance." Congress reserved for itself the authority to make regulations for the Library and decisions about how its budget would be used. A Joint Committee on the Library, to be composed of members of both houses, was established to decide how appropriations for new purchases should be spent. The privilege of borrowing books was extended to the president of the United States and the vice-president, but no one was permitted to take a map from the Library room.

The first Library of Congress took direction from President Thomas Jefferson, who probably knew more about books than any other American political figure of his day. He provided the Joint Committee on the Library with a list of additional titles needed to make the Library a useful reference collection for statesmen. This list guided additional purchases made from the initial appropriation of $5,000 and five supplemental appropriations of $1,000 each, allocated between 1806 and 1811.

President Jefferson appointed a political ally, John James Beckley, the clerk of the House of Representatives, to be the first librarian of Congress. Like most jobs in the federal government, the office of librarian of Congress was then considered a clerical position and was given to political supporters, a policy which continued until the late 1800s. Beckley, who retained his position as clerk, divided his pay as librarian with another clerk who took charge of the books and prepared the first catalog of the Library's holdings. After Beckley's death in 1807, Jefferson appointed Patrick Magruder, Beckley's successor as clerk of the House, to the position of librarian. Magruder took no particular interest in the collections of the Library and resigned both positions in 1815 when he could not account for $20,000 in expenditures.

Destruction and Reconstitution

By 1812, when war broke out again with Great Britain, the Library of Congress had grown to 905 titles in 3,000 volumes. The Joint Committee on the Library had spent a total of about $15,000 on the collection. The books were arranged

During the War of 1812, British troops captured the city of Washington and burned the U.S. Capitol. Much of the Library's 3,000-volume collection, which was housed in the Capitol, was destroyed.

by general subjects. The largest category consisted of history and biography, with 248 editions; law was the second largest group, with 204 titles. There were 105 books on geography and related subjects, 33 different dictionaries, and the famous *Encyclopéaedie* (comprising 35 volumes) of the French philosopher Denis Diderot. The Library had also received several reading editions of plays, poetry, and novels through gifts from members of Congress and various other individuals. Librarian Beckley had encouraged authors and publishers of new American editions to donate copies of their works, pledging to display them prominently in the Library and to note them in future catalogs. The Library of Congress was already something more than a practical reference collection for members of Congress.

Then, in August 1814, disaster struck. Just months before the end of the War of 1812, British troops invaded Washington and set fire to all public buildings except Blodget's Hotel, which housed the Post Office and the Patent

Office. The Capitol was virtually destroyed. A significant number of the books in the Library of Congress burned with it, although some volumes were hauled to safety before enemy soldiers entered the building. A young British army officer wrote later with regret that "doors, chairs, consumable parts, the library and its contents" were used to start the fire in an upper room of the Senate wing. The British justified their actions by pointing to similar acts by an American force that had raided the site of present-day Toronto, Ontario, (then a British colony). To Americans, however, the destruction of the capital by their former rulers seemed a retaliation for the success of American independence. After considering the idea of moving the capital to an older and more populous city, Congress defiantly determined to remain in Washington and reconstruct the public buildings.

An opportunity to rebuild the collections of the Library of Congress came shortly after the Capitol was destroyed: Toward the end of 1814, Thomas Jefferson, who was in retirement at Monticello and in need of money, offered

In 1815 Congress purchased President Jefferson's personal library of 6,487 volumes to help rebuild the Library's collection, which had been destroyed by the British. Jefferson's collection included many philosophy and history books such as these by the ancient Roman statesman Cicero and the Roman historian Tacitus.

to sell his personal library to Congress. His library, the finest and largest in the country at the time, numbered 6,487 volumes. Despite the objections of Jefferson's political opponents, who found fault with the nature of the former president's collection (some thought it was "too philosophical" and "irreligious" and contained too many books in foreign languages), Congress voted to purchase the entire library for $23,950. Ten horse-drawn carts delivered the books to Washington in early 1815. They were put on temporary shelves in Blodget's Hotel, where Congress met until the Capitol was sufficiently rebuilt.

The purchase of Jefferson's library allowed his far-ranging, singular intellect to give shape to the reconstituted Library of Congress. The new librarian of Congress, George Watterston, who was appointed by President James Madison in 1815, chose to adopt, with some alterations, Jefferson's personal system of book classification. This complex method of subject arrangement was based on Francis Bacon's system of knowledge, which was classified according to the three faculties of science—memory, reason, and imagination—and was very confusing to most users. However, the system remained in force until the early 20th century.

The addition of Jefferson's distinguished collection of books contributed to the growing public recognition of the Library of Congress as a national

George Watterston, librarian of Congress from 1815 to 1829, worked to increase the Library's holdings and to gain recognition for the idea of a national library.

collection. By 1816, borrowing privileges had been extended to members of the Supreme Court, the attorney general, and the diplomatic corps. In the years following the War of 1812, a new spirit of nationalism emerged in American art, literature, and education, and many people began to compare Congress's library with the great national libraries of Europe.

Librarian Watterston did all he could to gain recognition of the Library as a "great national repository" and even referred to it as the "Library of the United States." Like Beckley, he encouraged authors and publishers to donate copies of new publications. Although his relations with the Joint Committee on the Library were never smooth, he nevertheless managed to get powerful, tightfisted members to report to their colleagues "the absolute necessity of an extensive and judiciously selected library" and to recommend increases in appropriations for the purchase of books. During his tenure he also managed to gain from them a regular salary for the librarian of Congress ($1,000 a year) and authorization to employ a full-time assistant (to be paid $800 annually). The gains reflected the librarian's increased role as a reference source for the members of Congress, who increasingly requested "facts, dates, passages, acts, official communications, and even lines of poetry." Despite his service and accomplishments, Watterston was removed from his post in 1829 when President Andrew Jackson took office and replaced most government clerks with his own appointees.

Noble Quarters in the Capitol and the New Law Library

In 1824 the Library of Congress had been moved from the attic of the north wing of the Capitol to a large room in the center of the building, a site it would occupy until the end of the century. This impressive architectural space, which commanded remarkable views to the west and northwest, was considered the most beautiful room in Washington. The Library quickly became a popular site for visitors and a source of national pride. The new setting, however, also drew attention to the shortcomings of the Library of Congress's holdings. In 1826, historian Jared Sparks wrote that the Library of Congress's collection of American history was "exceedingly meager, containing nothing but the commonest books." However, "on the subject of American politics," Sparks noted, "it is full, particularly to the year 1808, when Mr. Jefferson left the government. It was his habit to preserve pamphlets and papers, and they are all deposited in this library."

Congress established a separate 2,000-volume law library in 1832. The Law Library, shown here around the year 1900 when it was located in the basement of the Capitol, was originally housed in a room near the Supreme Court's chambers.

A clear indication of Congress's growing reliance on the Library of Congress was its decision in 1832 to establish a separate law collection. Although the Law Library remained part of the Library of Congress, some 2,000 law books (including more than 600 from Jefferson's library) were removed from the general collection and placed in a separate room near the Supreme Court's chambers in the Capitol. The supervision and regulation of the law collection were transferred to the Court's justices, who soon extended borrowing privileges to lawyers arguing cases before them. (In 1830 Congress had formally extended library privileges to the members of the president's cabinet.)

By 1836 the Library of Congress had grown to a collection of roughly 24,000 volumes. This was eight times the holdings of the Library in 1812 and four times the number of books purchased from President Jefferson. Nevertheless, a report by the Joint Committee on the Library in 1836 pointed to the somewhat embarrassing evidence that the King's Library in Paris held almost a half million books; the Vatican Library, 400,000; the Russian Imperial Library in St. Petersburg, 300,000; and the British Museum, 180,000. Senator William C. Preston of Virginia, the chairman of the Joint Committee on the Library, urged his colleagues to substantially increase the holdings of the Library of Congress by purchasing the famous 25,000-volume library of the Russian nobleman and collector, Count Dimitrî Petrovich Buturlin. His proposal, which would instantly have doubled the size of the Library of Congress, was defeated in the Senate by one vote.

The Joint Committee's report was nevertheless significant and implied that the Library of Congress was at a crossroads in its development. The committee suggested that it was difficult to limit the Library's collection to a purely reference function. It pointed to an implied responsibility for the general spread of learning in the country, insisting in its report that the foundations of American government rested on the "aggregate intelligence of the citizens." For the moment these views were probably too sweeping and suggested too much additional responsibility for Congress at a time when the nation was uncertain about its own direction. In 1836, the country—and especially Congress—was absorbed in a national election and the question of whether Texas ought to be admitted to the Union.

In two other significant areas, however, Congress expanded the Library's role as a national repository. In July 1840, the Frenchman Alexandre Vattemare urged Congress to participate in the system of international exchanges of duplicate copies of books and official documents that he had organized in Europe. Six years later Congress passed the copyright law of 1846, which for the first time required applicants to submit three copies of their works to the government—one of which was to be deposited in the Library of Congress. (Congress had first recognized the need for copyright—the author's right to make and dispose of copies of an original work—when it passed "An Act for the Encouragement of Learning" in 1790.) The copyright law of 1846 proved ineffective, however, owing to the absence of measures for its enforcement, and the international exchange program was soon transferred to the Department of State. Watterston's successor as librarian of Congress, John S. Meehan, though industrious in serving the members of Congress, offered no support to these initiatives. Still, by broadening the Library's responsibilities, Congress had established new directions for the Library's growth as a national institution.

Fire and Civil War

By 1851 the Library of Congress's holdings had grown to approximately 50,000 volumes and were increasing at the rate of 1,800 a year. It was judged by experts to be a collection of great value, even if, as one commentator observed, it had been "collected by different committees . . . without any continued system" and "exhibited quite curiously the whims of Congresses and Congressmen." Its primary purpose and mission continued to be to serve the Congress, and the substantive decisions concerning it, including the selection of titles for purchase, were made by the Joint Committee on the Library. With the opening of the public library of the Smithsonian Institution in 1846, and its growth to some 10,000 volumes by 1850, there seemed even less justification for the Library of Congress to assume the larger role of a great national library.

Debate about the Library's future role was interrupted at mid-century by a catastrophic event. On Christmas Eve, 1851, a fire destroyed 35,000 volumes—roughly two-thirds of the books in the Library—as well as most of its map collection, three portraits by the painter Gilbert Stuart (of Washington, Adams, and Jefferson), and several other works of art. A congressional

During John Meehan's 31-year tenure as librarian of Congress, a fire—started on Christmas Eve, 1851—destroyed almost two-thirds of the Library's collection. Approximately a third of the books that had been bought from Jefferson were saved by fire fighters.

The library of the Smithsonian Institution in the 1860s. The Smithsonian Institution began to assemble a reference library, primarily of science books, in 1848. In 1866 it transferred its 40,000-volume collection to the Library of Congress.

THE SMITHSONIAN LIBRARY ROOM.

investigation soon determined that the flames had originated in chimney flues of committee rooms under the principal Library room. According to Thomas U. Walter, architect of the Capitol, the fire had spread as a result of "timbers which formed the alcoves of the Library having been inserted in the chimney flues." Librarian Meehan was not blamed; he had in fact taken unusual precautions, prohibiting the use of fireplaces and even candles and lamps in the reading room. Some valuable volumes (including approximately one-third of Jefferson's library) were saved by the efforts of fire fighters, and the Law Library, which had grown to 20,000 volumes, escaped damage.

Congress appropriated $75,000 to replace the books that had been destroyed or damaged and $72,500 (increased later to $93,000) to reconstruct the Library rooms. Gifts poured in from foreign nations and private individuals, and Meehan dutifully rebuilt the collections. The Library was replaced and rebuilt in elegant fashion without much regard to its future—at a time when the nation had just doubled in size as a consequence of the admission of Texas to the Union (1845), the settlement of the Oregon boundary (1846), and the Mexican cession following the Mexican War (1848).

In 1861, Meehan, then 71 years old and identified with the Democratic party, was removed by the new Republican president, Abraham Lincoln. Lincoln replaced him with John G. Stephenson, a 33-year-old physician from Terre Haute, Indiana, whose principal qualification was his service to the Republican party in the election of 1860. As one party insider observed after discussing the appointment with the president, "the Dr [Stephenson] is not heavy mettal but he has worked hard for us & is poor and can hand down books to M[embers of] C[ongress] as well & as gracefully as any one . . . " By this time the librarian of Congress commanded a salary of $2,160 and a staff of three assistants, a messenger, and two laborers. The Library's holdings had grown to 70,000 volumes, making it the fourth largest library in the United States.

Stephenson almost immediately discovered inadequacies in the Library's holdings and operations. He set out to rid the Library's books and furnishings of accumulated dirt and soot and attempted to introduce new efficiency and economies into the Library's operations. In 1864, however, he abruptly resigned his position, possibly as a result of a transaction in which the Library's London agent was defrauded. Stevenson's housekeeping extended to removals of several library employees, but to his credit he brought in Ainsworth Rand Spofford, a Cincinnati publisher and journalist, and a native of New Hampshire, to be his first assistant librarian.

The Spofford Era

Spofford had charge of the day-to-day management of the Library under Stephenson and then was appointed by President Lincoln to replace him as librarian of Congress. Though a firm advocate of the Republican party's principles, he had taken no active role in politics and was more influenced in his life by the works of Ralph Waldo Emerson and other New England writers of the mid-19th century. Like George Watterston, Spofford was first and foremost a bookman, committed to the goal of transforming the Library of Congress into a great national library. Unlike Watterston, however, he possessed keen political instincts and waged a well-calculated campaign in pursuit of his objective. Spofford's forceful intellect and personality had much to do with his success, but most important, he was the right man for the times. He took full advantage of the renewed sense of national will and purpose that emerged after the Civil War (1861–65) and made skillful appeals to national interest and congressional pride to advance his cause.

Ainsworth Spofford, appointed librarian of Congress by President Abraham Lincoln in 1864, had the entire copyright process transferred to the Library from the Patent Office. Spofford, who served for 32 years, committed himself to transforming the Library into a great institution.

Overcrowding was one of Librarian Spofford's major concerns in the 1870s. The new wings added to the Library room were soon filled with books and papers, and Spofford used the growth of the collections to champion the construction of a separate building for the Library.

In just five years, from 1865 to 1870, Spofford redirected the Library's future. He had the entire copyright process and previous copyright depositories (the Patent Office in the Department of the Interior, for example) transferred to the Library, secured two large collections that made the Library the largest and most important in the nation, and gained a large appropriation from Congress for the expansion of the Library's quarters in the Capitol. The Library's shelf space for books tripled in these five years, and its holdings grew from 82,000 to 237,000 volumes.

Spofford persuaded Congress to insert in new copyright legislation of 1865 a provision requiring that "a printed copy of every book, pamphlet, map, chart, musical composition, print, engraving, or photograph, for which copyright shall be secured" be transmitted free of charge to the Library of Congress. The more comprehensive copyright law of 1870 transferred all authority for the issuance and recording of copyrights to the librarian of Congress. The 1870 law further specified that two copies of the work for which copyright was sought were to be deposited in the Library, and, for the first time, set penalties for failure to do so. The new provision had the desired effect: Between 1870 and 1896 the Library received 371,636 books, 257,153 periodicals, 289,617 pieces of music, 73,817 photographs, 95,249 prints, and 48,048 maps as copyright deposits.

By an act of April 5, 1866, which reflected an agreement between Spofford and Joseph Henry, secretary of the Smithsonian Institution, the entire library of the Smithsonian was transferred to the Library of Congress. By this time the Smithsonian collection contained some 40,000 volumes and was particularly valuable in scientific areas, linguistics, bibliography, statistics, voyages and travels, and works pertaining to the fine arts. The Library of Congress also inherited the Smithsonian's exchange program, which was incorporated in a new policy on international exchanges that Congress established in 1867.

The transfer of the Smithsonian's library resolved the question of which institution would become the national library of the United States. The Smithsonian determined to concentrate on its scientific research and publications programs. By the act of transfer, it should be noted, the Smithsonian Institution received the same use and borrowing privileges provided the members of Congress; public access to its "Deposit" was specified in the agreement.

In 1867 Spofford convinced Congress to provide $100,000 for the purchase of the library of Washington publisher Peter Force, thereby gaining for the Library of Congress the finest private collection of materials relating to the early history of the United States. Force's library contained 22,529 books, about 1,000 volumes of newspapers, almost 40,000 pamphlets, more than 1,000 rare maps, several atlases, 429 volumes of important manuscripts, and a valuable collection of early printed books dating to the 15th and 16th centuries. The early American materials were substantially increased and enriched in 1882 when Dr. Joseph Toner, a Washington physician, donated his extensive collections to the Library.

Spofford had gained the space to accommodate these important acquisitions in 1865, when Congress allocated $160,000 for the expansion of the Library's quarters. Wings were added to the north and south ends of Thomas Walter's magnificent "fireproof" Library Room of 1852, and, though less ornamented than the original room, they were also constructed entirely of iron and stone. The new wings provided more than 26,000 feet of shelving space, room for about 210,000 books.

The additional space quickly filled up as a consequence of the 1870 copyright legislation and because of the Library's important acquisitions. Books and papers accumulated in corners and on surfaces in the Library Room, as well as in corridors, attics, and even the crypt below the basement under the rotunda of the Capitol. Although new staff were hired to catalog and manage the collections, there was no separate space for the preparation and storage of new books and materials. The clutter, noise, and confusion, Spofford informed the Joint Committee, made the reading room "an unfit place for students."

Beginning in 1871, Spofford carefully used the highly visible growth of the institution's collections to advocate a separate building for the Library of Congress. In 1886, President Grover Cleveland signed a bill providing for the construction of a new building across from and to the east of the Capitol grounds. This law, as Spofford knew, ensured that the Library of Congress would become a great national library.

Toward the close of his career, Spofford, like so many great figures, fell victim to the consequences of his successes. The growth of the Library's collections and staff—and of the federal government itself—had substantially increased his official duties. He had difficulty keeping up with paperwork, especially the copyright accounts, and was unable to make progress in cataloging the collections, an area in which he took particular interest from the outset of his tenure. (Congress had not appropriated money to hire a register of copyrights who could assist the librarian with the paperwork, thus enabling the librarian to devote more time to the catalog.) In addition, demand for services from the Library of Congress was growing, primarily from a constituency that should have been the most understanding of Spofford's accomplishments—the community of American libraries and librarians. Librarians, like others in the workplace drawn from the educated middle classes, found a new identity and self-importance in the late 19th century as the concept of profession emerged. The American Library Association (ALA), founded in 1876 to represent "professional librarians" and to promote their interests, had become influential and ambitious, and it wanted a voice in the Library's future. Preoccupied with his own work and plans for the new building, Spofford neglected to take sufficient notice of this new constituency. In hearings held in 1896, the year before the Library moved to its new quarters, the ALA sent an array of prominent members to Capitol Hill to lobby in favor of extensive new services to the nation's libraries—centralized cataloging, interlibrary loans, and a national union catalog listing the titles and locations of books found in libraries throughout the country—services that, the ALA argued, the Library of Congress should provide.

The ALA succeeded in portraying Spofford, then 72 years old, as the symbol of what was not modern and up-to-date. On July 1, 1897, the new president, William McKinley, appointed a new librarian of Congress. Spofford, ever faithful to the Library, accepted the position of chief assistant librarian, which he held from 1897 until his death in 1908.

Ainsworth Rand Spofford's tenure as librarian of Congress lasted 32 years. At its conclusion the congressional library had indeed become the national library of the United States as well as the Library of Congress. Unlike others then and now, he saw no contradiction in the dual nature and multiple functions of the Library. As John Y. Cole, the director of the Center for the Book at the Library of Congress and a Spofford authority, has observed, "He felt, as did Thomas Jefferson, that a comprehensive collection covering all subjects was as important to Congress as it was to scholars and the general public."

Architects John Smithmeyer and Paul Pelz's 1888 drawing of the proposed great hall for the new library. The magnificence of the structure's ornate architectural detail was echoed by its sheer size—the building encompassed an entire city block.

THREE

Growth and Transformation: The Nation's Library, 1897–1987

On July 31, 1897, the old Library in the Capitol was closed, and over the next three months the collections were moved to the new Library building. More than 750,000 books, 200,000 pamphlets, and 50,000 maps and charts, as well as thousands of other items, were carefully removed from rooms and corridors throughout the Capitol—from the dome to the crypt. The contents were transported by hand and cart to shelves in the recently completed structure across the Capitol grounds. This extensive operation was accomplished without significant loss or theft, at a total cost of $5,104.10 for labor and materials.

The monumental new residence of the Library of Congress was the embodiment in marble and stone of the concept of a national library, an idea which had inspired so many Americans in the 19th century. Its architecture, modeled after that of the Italian Renaissance, a great age of learning, gave

Construction of the new Library in 1891. The building was completed in 1897 and could hold more than 2 million books.

time-sanctioned form and meaning to the larger public role now assigned to the Library. It was now to be, in President William McKinley's words, "the national treasure-house of knowledge." The new Library was constructed of the finest materials and decorated ornately with murals, sculptures, and other works of art symbolic of the learning and culture of the great civilizations of the world. This confident statement of purpose in art and architecture also announced the nation's rise to world power and signaled a new emphasis on education and culture.

The new Library, constructed at a cost of $6 million over a period of 8 years, was a modified version of the original plan, selected in an 1873 design competition, of architects John Smithmeyer and Paul Pelz, who had consulted Spofford on the practical aspects of accommodating library functions. The final plans, however, reflected the ideas of several other architects and engineers, as well as those of the Joint Committee on the Library. The new structure was nevertheless harmonious and unified. It encompassed an entire city block, measuring 470 feet (in front) by 340 feet on the ground. By comparison the full extent of the original U.S. Capitol, completed in 1827, had been 335 feet in front.

In a sense, the scale and grandeur of the new Library overstated the degree to which the concept of the national library and "treasure-house" had been accepted by the federal government in the 1890s. The building, like the U.S. Capitol, was a national statement of purpose, intended in large part to gain the respect and admiration of the world. From the viewpoint of economics, the building's magnificence was made possible only by the great increases in the nation's wealth in the late 19th century, which allowed the government to procure the best materials and the services of the finest artists and craftsmen. The total costs for the construction of the building were actually less than the original allocation of 1889—a tribute not only to the management of the Army Corps of Engineers, which had charge of the construction, but also to the purchasing power of the American dollar worldwide.

When the new building opened on November 1, 1897, John Russell Young

Artisans work with stucco during the construction of the new Library. Congress authorized the hiring of the finest craftsmen and artists to design and decorate the building.

41

occupied the spacious office of the librarian of Congress. A career diplomat appointed by President William McKinley, Young had an unusual opportunity at the outset of his tenure to give shape and direction to the institution. In funding legislation of 1897, the Library had received authorization to expand from 42 to 108 employees. The same legislation had given the librarian extensive powers over the operations of the Library and had increased his annual salary to $5,000. Even though the 66 newly funded positions did not fall under civil service regulations that applied to most nonpolitical government jobs, Young determined to fill these appointments on the basis solely of merit. Young recruited experienced librarians and others with expertise in special fields to head new organizational units approved by Congress. These units consisted of catalog, copyright, manuscript, music, and periodical departments; the reading room; the art gallery; the hall of maps and charts; the congressional reference library (which remained in the Capitol); and the Law Library. In making his selections, Young took into consideration the geographical backgrounds of candidates, thinking it appropriate that the Library reflect its nature as a national institution in the composition of its staff. He also made it a point to hire women and blacks. During his tenure as librarian, one-quarter of the Library of Congress's employees were female and 10 percent were black. (One of his appointments was the black poet Paul Laurence Dunbar.) Young assigned the training of new personnel to his chief assistant librarian, Ainsworth Spofford, who had had much to do with planning for the new Library.

The great spaces of the new building, which had storage capacity for more than 2 million books, stirred Young's ambitions for the Library. He quickly gave priority to efforts to increase and improve the quality of the collections. He convinced Congress to raise the annual appropriation for new acquisitions from $4,000 for 1898 to $15,000 for 1899. In addition he organized an international effort that utilized the nation's foreign service to secure books and manuscripts representative of other cultures and introduced special programs and services for the blind.

Young died in January 1899, having served a brief but eventful term of 18 months. His achievement in setting the Library on its new course, strengthening its identity as a national institution, is perhaps best measured by the events surrounding the naming of his successor. The following month President McKinley nominated a political friend, a member of the House of Representatives, to be the eighth librarian of Congress. Within two weeks the Senate Committee on the Library reported negatively on this nomination and forced the president to submit the name of a candidate with the proper qualifications to serve.

The Putnam Era

Young's successor, Herbert Putnam, took office on April 5, 1899; he was to hold the position of librarian of Congress for the next 40 years. Born into a well-known New York publishing family, Putnam was educated at Harvard and Columbia where he studied law. He served as the librarian of the Minneapolis Athenaeum and later of that city's public library, which he had a large role in establishing. At the time of his appointment as librarian of Congress, he was director of the Boston Public Library, then the largest library in the country. As a librarian, Putnam had been a modernizer, particularly effective in improving services to readers and in generating public interest in the library as a cultural institution.

Putnam came to his new position with clear ideas about the Library of Congress's mission and knowledge of its inadequacies. Soon after taking office, he wrote that the Library was not fulfilling its primary duty to Congress nor its secondary duties to other offices of the federal government and to scholarship. "It is rendering effective service as a reference library for the District of Columbia; but such a service scarcely justifies a seven-million-dollar plant, maintained at an expenditure of over a quarter of a million dollars a year." The

Herbert Putnam, librarian of Congress from 1899 to 1939, organized the Library's collections by reclassifying and recataloging the holdings. The alphanumeric system he instituted remains the standard system of classification for most libraries today.

43

principal reasons for the Library's failings were the large backlog in cataloging and the lack of effective finding aids to the collections. Without a thorough knowledge of the Library's extensive holdings, a reader could not retrieve information with full confidence that it was complete and up-to-date. To compound matters, the Library's collections were rapidly increasing, but only one-third of its current holdings had even been cataloged.

Putnam convinced Congress of the pressing need for a new and systematic effort to reclassify and recatalog the Library's entire holdings. In 1900 he received funding for 81 new positions to help accomplish this and for 15 new clerks for the Copyright Office. He also gained a substantial increase in the Library's appropriation for acquisitions. In an effort to make the institution more efficient, Putnam reorganized his staff into 18 administrative units that reflected the principal areas of the Library's work and services.

The campaign to gain control over the Library's collections went forward immediately. The Library adopted a card catalog system (whereby each item was recorded on a three-by-five-inch card and filed according to title, author, and subject). This system enabled the Library to catalog its holdings with greater ease and efficiency for the purposes of Congress and the public and for the Library's own internal supervision.

The Library implemented a new classification system to replace the Jeffersonian system it had been using throughout the 19th century. The new classification employed a combination of letters and numbers to organize the books by subject into 20 major classes of knowledge. (Books relating to world history, for example, were assigned the letter *D*; modern history was placed within the numerals 204 to 725.) This alphanumeric system made possible greater accuracy in organizing and identifying the Library's extensive holdings. The Library of Congress system soon became, and still remains, the standard system of classification used in large libraries throughout the United States. (The Dewey Decimal Classification, an alternative system that divides knowledge into 10 main classes, is the method used by most elementary and secondary school libraries and by small public libraries in the United States.)

Underlying Putnam's efforts was his belief that the Library of Congress should be "a bureau of information for the entire country" and the center of a national library system. A leader in the library profession, he saw that the improvements and efficiencies that he was introducing at the Library of Congress could be widely applied. The growth of public libraries in the United States in the late 19th century was a phenomenon justly celebrated—by 1901 there were more than 5,000 nationwide. But the nation's libraries needed centralized services if they were to meet the needs of readers and researchers

The Library's card catalog division, about 1915. In keeping with Putnam's notion that the Library of Congress should be "a bureau of information for the entire country," in 1901 the Library made its catalog cards available to other libraries for a nominal fee.

and avoid duplication of effort and expense. In 1901 the Library of Congress began to make copies of its printed catalog cards available for sale to other libraries—a service that quickly became indispensable to smaller libraries. It also commenced a program of interlibrary loans—loaning books in its collections to other libraries by mail so that readers could use them without having to travel to Washington. To further facilitate research throughout the country, the Library provided complete sets of its catalog cards to 25 official libraries of deposit.

The first decade of the Putnam era was also noteworthy for its important acquisitions. In 1903, President Theodore Roosevelt ordered that the historical archives of the Department of State, which included the papers of the Continental Congress and those of Presidents Washington, Jefferson, and Madison, be transferred to the Library of Congress. Other departments in the executive branch were instructed to make similar transfers. The following year the Library initiated a program to copy documents relating to American history held in foreign archives. It also purchased an important private collection of

45

Employees of the Library's Legislative Reference Service in 1925. Congress established the Service in 1915 to assist members in gathering information while drafting legislation.

Benjamin Franklin's diplomatic correspondence. Collections of international significance—notably an entire library devoted to Russian literature and culture (once used by Russian revolutionary Vladimir Lenin) and large numbers of Japanese and Chinese materials—were purchased. In addition the Library launched an ambitious program of bibliographical and documentary publications.

The growth of the Library of Congress in the first decade of the 20th century firmly established it as an institution of national and international importance. By 1910 it had become the third largest library in the world. The death two years earlier of Ainsworth Spofford served to emphasize the dramatic progress. Since 1897, when he had stepped down as librarian of Congress, the number of Library employees had tripled. When he had assumed the position in 1864 Spofford had inherited a staff of seven in the old Library quarters in the Capitol; when he retired as librarian 32 years later he still had only 16 employees working exclusively on Library matters (26 other employees worked full-time on copyright business). Although the Library's achievements in the first decade of the 20th century were encouraged by America's rise to world power and responsibility, they were also a testament to Spofford's vision and patient planning and to Putnam's leadership.

The expansion of the Library's resources and services would not have occurred without large increases in funding by Congress. As members of the

House and the Senate continued to support the growth of the Library, they began to demand more in return. The Library's expansion in the early 20th century reflected growth in every area of national life and the nation's greater international role, which substantially increased Congress's responsibilities and burdens. The experience of several state governments, notably that of Wisconsin, which in 1901 had drawn on the resources of its state library and university to create a legislative reference bureau, suggested to many members that a similar organization on the national level was necessary to assist Congress in its work of legislating. The Wisconsin bureau had researched and even drafted bills for the review of legislators, but a consensus gradually developed in the Senate and the House that a congressional reference bureau should provide only data and information—not actual legislative services. Upon hearing that the Congress was considering such a proposal, Putnam worked closely with members to suggest ways to set up such an organization within the Library and, as a result, in 1915 the Legislative Reference Service (LRS) was established. The appropriations legislation authorized "the Librarian of Congress to employ competent persons to prepare such indexes, digests, and compilations of law as may be required for Congress and other official use." In convincing the Congress to establish the LRS within the Library of Congress, Putnam skillfully gained control of the new service.

In 1921 the federal government transferred the Declaration of Independence and the U.S. Constitution from the State Department to the Library of Congress, thus securing—in the eyes of the public—the Library's position as a great national institution.

47

In the period between World Wars I and II, the Library's position as a great national institution was further solidified. Public recognition of its preeminent stature was firmly established when the Declaration of Independence and the Constitution were transferred from the Department of State in 1921. The documents were placed on display in the Library in a formal ceremony presided over by President Calvin Coolidge. (The documents were later transferred to the National Archives and Records Administration in 1953.) The Library's prestige as a national institution was reinforced by its sheer size. By 1928 its collections had reached 3.5 million books and 10 million items, and its staff had increased to 737 employees.

End of the Putnam Era

During the 1920s the Library's central place in the cultural life of the nation began to attract several large private donations and bequests. The largest was the gift and endowment of philanthropist Elizabeth Sprague Coolidge, who donated funds to pay for the construction of an auditorium in the Library and to endow performances of chamber music. In 1925, Congress passed the Library of Congress Trust Fund Act to enable the Library to receive this and other private gifts. Some of the gifts were made to broaden ongoing Library programs—notably, for the program to copy documents relating to American history held in European archives and for the improvement of the Library's bibliographic services. But beginning in 1927, gifts were also made to establish chairs and consultant positions within the Library. Putnam sought these donations for two purposes: to boost the salaries of the Library's division chiefs and experts so that they were comparable to those paid to university professors and to provide positions for experienced specialists, who would share their expertise with researchers. With these additional resources Putnam expected to improve the Library's capabilities in interpreting its collections to the public.

By this time Putnam was less interested in directing the Library's resources to the technical matters of librarianship and more concerned with the institution's role in the intellectual and cultural life of the nation and in its international prestige. He regularly invited writers, officials, and other dignitaries to the "Librarian's Round Table," a gathering for lunch and intellectual conversation over which Putnam presided. In 1930 he gained from Congress an appropriation of $1.5 million to purchase (at half the market value) retired scientist Otto Vollbehr's collection of 3,000 rare 15th-century books—the

In 1930 the Library purchased from scientist Otto Vollbehr (right) a collection of 15th-century books, which included a vellum copy of the Gutenberg Bible, for $1.5 million. The acquisition was considered to be one of Librarian Putnam's greatest triumphs.

earliest and most famous of which was one of three surviving original vellum copies of the Gutenberg Bible, the first book to be printed using movable type. In 1935 the Library accepted the collector and philanthropist Gertrude Clarke Whittall's gift of musical instruments, including five violins made by 17th-century master violin maker Antonio Stradivari, and her endowment to fund the construction of a display room and performances using these instruments. Other notable gifts, received in 1928 and 1938, established what today is the Archive of Folk Song (now part of the Archive of Folk Culture) and the Hispanic Division for studies in Spanish- and Portuguese-speaking cultures. To a considerable extent the Library was being reshaped by these donations, which went beyond, and in some ways diverted attention from, its traditional areas of concern.

Putnam continued to control all matters relating to the Library, which by this time had expanded to 35 divisions, and to determine its priorities. In 1939, when he was 78 years old, the division chiefs were still reporting directly to him. The operations of the Library depended on the attention he was able or

Collector and philanthropist Gertrude Clarke Whittall donated three violins, a viola, and a cello—made by Antonio Stradivari in the 17th century—to the Library in 1935–36. Many of the Library's rare and special collections have been gifts from philanthropists.

willing to give them. This concentration of authority contributed to a decline in staff morale and to other dilemmas, including backlogs in the cataloging of collections and an acute need for additional shelf space—conditions Putnam had found and publicly deplored upon becoming librarian in 1899. His relations with Congress remained good, however. In 1930, having obtained land behind the Library's main building, he received an appropriation of $6.5 million from Congress for the construction of the "Annex" to provide additional shelf and work space. This building was opened in 1939, the year Putnam retired as librarian.

World War II and the Poet-Librarian

President Franklin D. Roosevelt's choice to succeed Putnam, Archibald MacLeish, was initially opposed as "unfit" by the leading organization of professional librarians, the American Library Association. By training a lawyer, and at the time of his appointment a distinguished poet and man of letters, MacLeish accepted President Roosevelt's offer to serve as librarian of Congress with reluctance, preferring to spend his full time writing poetry. In choosing MacLeish, the president put the poet's qualities as a leader and spokesman for democratic culture above his lack of experience in the technical aspects of librarianship. The world was at war, even though the United States was not yet an active participant. By 1939 many knowledgeable observers had come to believe that the future of Western civilization was at stake in the effort to defeat the forces of fascism.

MacLeish served only five years as librarian of Congress, but he left substantial accomplishments. He achieved these despite the hardships imposed on him and the Library by the demands of World War II. Within weeks after the Japanese attack on Pearl Harbor in December 1941, important materials, amounting to some 5,000 cases in 29 truckloads, were removed to safe storage outside the capital. The Declaration of Independence, the Constitution, the Bill

Archibald MacLeish, librarian of Congress during the World War II era, was a distinguished poet who expanded the Library's cultural programs, particularly in the areas of literature and poetry.

of Rights, the Gutenberg Bible, and the Library's Stradivarius violins were sent under military escort to Fort Knox, Kentucky. Like other civilian agencies of the federal government, the Library took on additional wartime responsibilities, notably in foreign language training and antipropaganda work. At the president's request, MacLeish himself took on added wartime roles, including the directorship of the Office of Facts and Figures, an agency established to serve as a central source of official information about the war effort.

With the outbreak of the war, the Library's role as a repository of great works of civilization suddenly took on an urgency. As MacLeish wrote in *Atlantic Monthly* in 1940, "Librarians are keepers . . . of the records of the human spirit—the records of men's watch upon the world and on themselves. In such a time as ours, when wars are made against the spirit and its works, the keeping of these records is itself a kind of warfare. The keepers, whether they so wish or not, cannot be neutral."

MacLeish inherited almost absolute power over an institution which by this time had an annual budget of $3 million, a staff of some 1,100, and collections that included almost 6 million books and pamphlets, almost a quarter of which had not been fully cataloged. He quickly gained funding from Congress to hire 50 new employees to attack the cataloging backlog, which was increasing at the rate of 30,000 items a year. He then turned his attention to the administrative disorder that had largely caused the backlog, reorganizing the Library into basic functional units and appointing able administrators to supervise them. A proponent of "government by discussion," MacLeish encouraged staff partic- ipation in all aspects of the Library's management and by the end of his tenure had secured substantial upgrades in status and pay for Library employees.

MacLeish gave new focus to the Library's work and purpose in his annual report for 1940. He inaugurated a program of fellowships to bring in scholars to assist the Library in its purchases, a program that lasted into the 1950s. He further invigorated the Library by expanding its cultural programs, particularly in the areas of literature and poetry.

The Postwar Period

In December 1944, MacLeish accepted appointment as assistant secretary of state for public and cultural relations. After contributing to the preparation of a draft charter for the United Nations the following year, he resumed his life as a full-time poet. He was succeeded as librarian by Luther H. Evans, chief assistant librarian since 1940. A political scientist, Evans came to his new position with administrative experience and knowledge of the Library and its operations. He had served as director of the Legislative Reference Service during 1939 and 1940, and, as chief assistant librarian and director of the newly formed Reference Department, he had played an important role in MacLeish's administrative reorganization.

Evans shared MacLeish's objectives and during his tenure as librarian attempted to carry out his predecessor's plans for the improvement as well as development of the Library. He also pursued a course recommended by President Harry S. Truman, who nominated him to be librarian in June 1945. The president told Evans that he wanted the Library "to give service to Congress, but . . . also to be 'the Library of the United States' and give increased service to the little libraries all over the country."

Evans's declared priorities were to strengthen the Library's foreign acquisitions and to secure budget increases that would enable it to serve the nation as a great cultural institution. He carefully mustered his arguments and justifications for a budget of $9.75 million for fiscal year 1947, an amount twice that appropriated for the previous year. However, Congress wanted to reduce government expenditures after the war ended in 1945 and only appropriated slightly more than $6 million. This figure contained substantial increases for the Copyright Office and the Legislative Reference Service (established as a

Librarian Luther H. Evans (left), Chief Justice Fred M. Vinson, and President Harry S. Truman participate in Constitution Day ceremonies on September 17, 1951, in the Library's Great Hall.

separate and largely independent unit within the Library by terms of the Legislative Reorganization Act of 1946), but it did not provide the substantial increase for acquisitions and new projects that Evans had requested.

Failure to gain Congress's full approval for his broad proposals did not, however, prevent Evans from implementing them. By improving international purchase and exchange arrangements, relying on microfilm photography (by which books and documents are reproduced on rolls of film) to gain copies of foreign materials, and actively seeking private gifts, he managed to increase the Library's holdings by 28 percent during his tenure. Cataloging procedures were simplified and improved; a Serial Record Division for cataloging periodicals and similar publications was set up; and the Library issued important bibliographical publications to guide libraries and scholarly communities. In 1949, in response to the growing demand from the public and from federal agencies for assistance in science and technical subjects, the Library established a separate Science Division.

Like MacLeish, Evans believed in democratic participation in the management of the Library and considered the morale of the Library staff an important ingredient of its effectiveness. To a considerable extent, however, decision making was kept in the librarian's office during his tenure. He put the Library ahead of other institutions by stating publicly that all members of his staff deserved "an equality of treatment on the basis of merit," even though there were no laws at that time that forced him to observe this policy. He further stated that there would be "no discrimination unrelated to the merits of a person's performance and his attitude based upon differences of sex, or of race, or of religion."

Evans held strong views on education, internationalism (an outlook that places international cooperation, especially in the area of economic and foreign policy, above consideration of national interest), and the free exchange of ideas, and he published them widely during his tenure as librarian. Like many of his generation he believed that a new world had to emerge after World War II. "Starved minds and starved spirits breed totalitarianism and madness just as bitterly and suddenly and inexorably as do hungry stomachs," he warned in 1949. He saw himself as a spokesman for universal values represented by the Library and made many speeches around the country, often attacking McCarthyism (methods employed by Senator Joseph McCarthy of Wisconsin in his campaign to identify communists and communist "sympathizers" within and without the federal government during the 1950s) and threats of censorship. These activities led many in Congress to conclude that he was not giving sufficient attention to the management of the Library. In 1953, he resigned as librarian to become director-general of the United Nations Educational, Scientific, and Cultural Organization (UNESCO), a post he held until 1958. He later served as director of a study group on federal libraries that recommended the transfer of the Library of Congress to the executive branch of government.

The Mumford Years

Evans's successor, L. Quincy Mumford, appointed by President Dwight D. Eisenhower in 1954, was the first, and to date the only, professionally trained librarian to serve as librarian of Congress. A native of North Carolina, Mumford had served on the staff of the New York Public Library from 1929 to 1945 and was the director of the Cleveland Public Library from 1945 to 1954. He was well acquainted with the Library of Congress, having been brought to Washington by Librarian MacLeish in 1940 – 41 to reorganize the processing divisions of the Library of Congress.

The Library's good relations with members of Congress had deteriorated under Mumford's predecessors. Restoring these was his first challenge. When

The 9th and 11th librarians of Congress, MacLeish (right) and L. Quincy Mumford, in 1956. MacLeish first brought Mumford, a professionally trained librarian, to Washington in 1940 to reorganize the processing divisions of the Library of Congress.

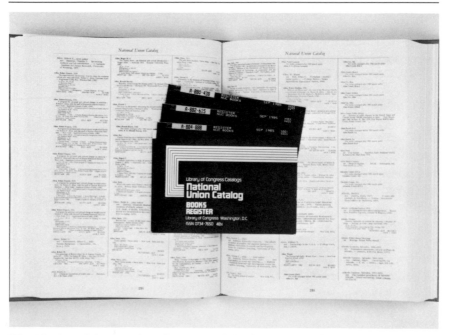

The National Union Catalog, a multivolume record of books housed in 2,500 research libraries across the country, is available in bound volumes and on microfiche.

he took office, the Library's appropriations requests were under fire. He was able to convince members of both houses, however, that the Library had to grow in order to serve effectively as the research arm of Congress. His skills of persuasion are easily measured—during his first 10 years as librarian the Library's appropriations went from $9.3 million to just above $24 million.

Mumford concentrated his efforts on the Library's chronic problems in cataloging and on the improvement of the Library's collections. During his long tenure he gained substantial increases in funding from Congress to attack the cataloging backlog. He launched the publication of the *National Union Catalog, Pre-1956 Imprints* (a multivolume series compiled from the card catalogs of participating libraries throughout North America) and oversaw the Library's transition to automation in cataloging. Similarly, the innovative concept of Cataloging in Publication (CIP)—whereby publishers forward prepublication information about new books to the Library so that cataloging can be accomplished in advance and then printed in the books—was explored during his tenure and eventually adopted (in 1973).

56

Mumford's tenure as librarian was not without controversy. In the early 1960s, a movement among major university libraries that was supported to an extent by the administration of John F. Kennedy pressed to have the Library of Congress officially designated the national library of the United States and transferred (except for the Legislative Reference Service) to the executive branch. Mumford countered with an artful defense, keeping the Library within the legislative branch. He argued that the Library was in a better position to secure the funding it needed within the legislative branch, which has the greatest leverage in budget matters. He would support the designation of the Library as the national library of the United States—but not if it interfered with his immediate objectives of gaining increased funding for an additional building for the Library and for national library functions. The Library was also under attack during Mumford's tenure because of its practices in the recruitment, training, and promotion of minorities, but the record clearly shows that during the Mumford years the Library of Congress was well in advance of other federal agencies in these areas.

During the Johnson and Nixon administrations in the 1960s and 1970s, the Library's dual nature was further defined by legislation. Under amendments to the Higher Education Act of 1965, the Library was authorized "to provide new and unparalleled services for the benefit of other libraries," including "acquiring as far as possible all library materials of value to scholarship that are currently published throughout the world" and "providing catalog information for these materials promptly." The National Program for Acquisitions and Cataloging (NPAC), formed under this legislation, has been particularly successful in coordinating the purchase and cataloging of foreign scholarly materials. Under the Legislative Reorganization Act of 1970, Congress greatly expanded the size and scope of the Legislative Reference Service, doubling the number of its employees, which at the time totaled 438. In the same legislation the Legislative Reference Service was renamed the Congressional Research Service (CRS).

Mumford's leadership was characterized by his careful, thoroughly professional approach to management and to the major issues that confronted the Library. The problems that would challenge his successors—such as computer automation and the preservation of deteriorating materials—were identified and addressed. The Library's pressing need for additional space was resolved by Congress in appropriations, beginning in 1965, of $123 million for the construction of the James Madison Memorial Library.

When Mumford retired on December 31, 1974, after 20 years of service, the Library of Congress had become a large government agency. Its dual nature, as Congress's library and the national library of the United States, was firmly established. Its collections had grown from 33 million to 74 million items, its staff from 1,564 to 4,250 people, and its annual expenditures from $9.4 million to $96.7 million. The Library of Congress had become not only the largest library in the world but also the largest library in human history.

Innovations of Librarian Boorstin, 1975–87

Mumford's successor was Daniel Boorstin, who was appointed librarian of Congress by President Gerald R. Ford in 1975. A historian, widely published with a particular interest in American technology, Boorstin introduced many innovations during his 12-year tenure, most in response to the significant technological and cultural changes of the late 20th century. When Boorstin became librarian in 1975, the number of people using the reading rooms of the Library of Congress was declining noticeably, reading skills were deteriorating in the nation's schools, and illiteracy rates among the general public were rising. These problems were alarming for a democratic society governed by the will of the voters. The new librarian also knew that the Library's advances in computer automation would eventually have the effect of reducing the amount of time readers and researchers needed to spend in the Library with books. He responded to these disturbing trends by developing various programs and ideas designed to expand the Library's readership and to reinforce the public's perception of the Library as a great national cultural center.

Acting in part on the recommendations of a task force he commissioned to provide him with a full-scale review of the institution, Boorstin took a new look at the Library—from the perspective of the reader and researcher. As a result, he brought about changes designed to increase the use of the Library's resources and to strengthen the Library's public image. He determined to open up the Library as an institution and promote it as a three-dimensional "multimedia encyclopedia." He placed reference librarians in the front lines of his campaign to direct readers quickly and efficiently to the information they needed. He developed plans for getting special materials to special constituencies: His most notable success in decentralizing the Library's collections was the placement of a branch of the Performing Arts Library as a theatrical and musical resource center in the John F. Kennedy Center for the Performing Arts, established in Washington, D.C., in 1971. He believed that the Library's theatrical and musical materials would be best utilized there. These attempts

The John F. Kennedy Center for the Performing Arts in Washington, D.C. In 1971 Librarian of Congress Daniel Boorstin succeeded in locating a branch of the Performing Arts Library in the Center. The branch library houses a 4,000-volume reference collection and audiovisual equipment.

to reorient the Library's reader services from the perspective of the reader were generally well received, and Boorstin's seemingly endless drive to innovate challenged the Library staff.

Having served as director of the Smithsonian's Museum of History and Technology (today the National Museum of American History) prior to coming to the Library, Boorstin brought with him an appreciation for the educational and promotional methods used by large public museums. He introduced many of these methods to the Library in an effort to improve its ability to explain its role and services to the general public. He pursued almost every opportunity to put the Library in the news and to enlarge its public constituency—traveling exhibitions of the Library's collections and visual aids were expanded, sales shops were made more attractive, even lunchtime folk music concerts were inaugurated. The public areas of the Library were redecorated and the Library's main building became a center for elegant gatherings of the nation's creative elite. To emphasize the value of exchanges between "those who collect, arrange, and preserve the raw materials of scholarship and the literary arts and those who reinterpret and vivify them anew for each generation," Boorstin formed a Council of Scholars, composed of well-known artists and scholars, including former secretary of state Henry Kissinger, historian Arthur Schlesinger, jr., and violinist Yehudi Menuhin. He also sought the advice of leaders in many related fields on "large intellectual questions affecting scholarship and public policy."

Of the several new projects launched during Boorstin's tenure as librarian, which ended with his retirement in 1987, perhaps the most significant was the Center for the Book. This organization, largely privately funded, was formed by legislation passed in October 1977 to stimulate public interest in the history and culture of the book and in reading. The importance of its work was forcefully stated by Librarian Boorstin when the Center was established:

> As the national library of a great free republic, we have a special inter-
> est to see that books do not go unread, that they are read by people of
> all ages and conditions, that books are not buried in their own dross,
> not lost from neglect or obscured from us by specious alternatives and
> synthetic substitutes. As the national library of the most technologically
> advanced nation on earth, we have a special duty, too, to see that the
> book is the useful, illuminating servant of all other technologies, and that
> all other technologies become the effective, illuminating acolytes of the
> book.

In its first decade the Center for the Book attempted to accomplish these goals in several ways. It sponsored lectures, exhibitions, and publications, and brought together leaders in various fields to discuss and deal with issues affecting the role of the book. The Center also promoted reading in the secondary schools and encouraged scholarly interest in the history of the book

Librarian Boorstin (left) and Chief Justice Warren Burger toast "the book" at a fund-raiser for the Center of the Book. Congress established the Center in 1977 to stimulate interest in the history of books and in reading.

Chief Justice William Rehnquist (left) swears in James H. Billington as the 13th librarian of Congress on September 14, 1987. Billington, who was appointed to the post by President Ronald Reagan (second from left), is exploring new technologies, such as the optical disk, to make the Library's collections more accessible throughout the country.

and in all aspects of printing. Several state and regional Centers for the Book were formed as affiliate organizations to assist the Library's Center in extending the reach of its programs.

The Thirteenth Librarian of Congress

In April 1987, President Ronald Reagan nominated James H. Billington to be the 13th librarian of Congress, and in July of that year the Senate approved the nomination. Prior to his appointment, the new librarian, a historian of Russian history and culture, had been the director of the Woodrow Wilson International Center for Scholars in Washington, D.C. In his initial observations on the Library and its future, Billington indicated his support for the initiatives of his predecessor while at the same time suggesting that the Library's great holdings should be probed more deeply and shared more broadly. He pointed to the potential of new technologies for making the Library's collections more accessible throughout the country, but he also cautioned that the Library's capacity to simply move information about would be of little value if it failed to take a leadership role "in helping turn information into knowledge and distill it all into some wisdom."

Librarian Billington reads to a group of children at the Family Reading Celebration in the Great Hall in 1988. The Library of Congress and a public television station were cosponsors of the event, which brought Washington-area children and their families to the Library.

FOUR

The Library of Congress Today

The Library of Congress, like most of the departments and bureaus of the federal government, reflects both the historical development of the Library as an institution and the specific legislation of past Congresses. It remains the congressional library but enjoys preeminence in the nation and the world as the national library of the United States. This dual role is not considered interrelated by some observers, notably professional librarians, but the two constituencies, Congress and the nation, have in fact shaped the unique character of the Library as it is known today.

In the 1920s and 1930s, the Library assumed the additional role of serving as a theater for musical performances, which it continues to an extent today. In the same period it extended its areas of interest to embrace aspects of American folk life, and since the beginning of the century, it has been a forerunner in the development of programs for the visually and physically impaired. The Library's various cultural programs and responsibilities nevertheless continue to reflect the principal collections it now maintains.

Jefferson, Adams, and Madison Buildings

Today the Library of Congress is housed principally in three major public buildings connected to one another and to the Capitol by underground passages. The oldest of the buildings, the new Library of 1897, was renamed the Thomas Jefferson Building in 1980 and remains a monument to the age that conceived and constructed it. At its center is the Main Reading Room, a great circular space measuring 125 feet high by 100 feet wide, which is covered by a dome. This room alone contains a reference collection of some 40,000 books. In conception and decoration the Main Reading Room forms a powerful symbol of the progress of human civilization. Stack areas containing shelves for books and other materials radiate from the Main Reading Room and are connected by a mechanical book railway to the other Library buildings. The Jefferson Building also houses a number of special reading rooms, such as the Rare Book and Special Collections Reading Room, the Local History and Genealogy Reading Room, and the European Division Reading Room.

The Annex of 1939, situated immediately behind the Jefferson Building, has been renamed the John Adams Building. This structure, though modest in comparison to the Thomas Jefferson Building, is a fine example of the art deco style of architecture inspired by the influential 1925 Paris exhibition of the decorative arts. Although intended to be purely functional and designed to contain needed work space and twice the shelf space available in the Jefferson

Pilgrims from Chaucer's Canterbury Tales *are depicted in a mural in the Library's John Adams Building, which was constructed in 1939. Some of the reference collections held in the John Adams Building include materials pertaining to all areas of sub-Saharan Africa and materials in the Japanese, Chinese, and Korean languages.*

The James Madison Memorial Library, which opened to the public in 1980, is the Library of Congress's newest and largest building. It houses administrative offices, nonbook collections, and several of the special collections, including the Prints and Photographs Division, the Manuscript Division, and the Music Division.

Building, the Annex was beautifully constructed. Its public spaces are imaginatively decorated with murals, notably of figures from Chaucer's *Canterbury Tales*, and with fine ornamental metalwork.

The newest building, the James Madison Memorial Library (in 1988 the largest library building in the world), is located directly across Pennsylvania Avenue from the Jefferson Building. Except for a spacious memorial hall containing a large statue of the fourth president and its scale, the Madison Building is essentially featureless. It is built in modular fashion with movable walls, and holds the distinction of having more floor space than any other federal office building except the Federal Bureau of Investigation building and the Pentagon. The Madison Building was opened to the public in 1980 and houses most of the Library's administrative offices and nonbook collections. It also contains the reading rooms and collections of several special collections divisions—among them the Manuscript, Prints and Photographs, and Music divisions—and an exhibition gallery.

In 1984, Congress appropriated $81.5 million to the office of the architect of the Capitol for the renovation and restoration of the Jefferson and the Adams buildings. This extensive project, scheduled for completion in 1993, encompasses the modernization of the structures to bring them into compliance with current building standards and to introduce new facilities and data communication lines equipment. The appropriation also included funds for the cleaning and restoration of the artwork and architectural details of the two historic buildings.

Office of the Librarian of Congress

The organization and management of the Library is in the hands of the librarian of Congress, who is appointed by the president of the United States subject to the confirmation of the Senate. The librarian reports to the Joint Committee of Congress on the Library, but his or her activities are not otherwise governed by specific legislation. In practice the librarian of Congress, whose budgets are reviewed and approved by Congress every year, maintains close relations with the Joint Committee on the Library, which usually is the Library's advocate within the Congress. In 1988 the annual appropriation for the Library was almost $248 million; the annual salary of the librarian, $82,500.

The librarian oversees the work of six departments: National Programs, the Law Library, the Copyright Office, the Congressional Research Service (all of which were established by acts of Congress), Processing Services, and Research Services. These 6 units oversee some 85 subdivisions.

The Library's National Programs department includes the exhibits office, which mounted "Nazi Book Burnings and the American Response" in 1988. The exhibit included pictures, manuscripts, cartoons, posters, and newspaper accounts of book burnings during World War II, and it was sponsored by the United States Holocaust Memorial Council.

Musicians perform on the Library's plaza in a concert sponsored by the American Folklife Center, which was established in 1976 to preserve and promote American culture.

National Programs

National Programs encompasses the Library's Information, Publishing, Educational Liaison, and Exhibits offices, as well as the Children's Literature Center, the American Folklife Center, and the National Library Service for the Blind and Physically Handicapped. All of these divisions are in some way involved in the Library's outreach programs to bring the Library to the American public. The Information Office is the Library's public affairs unit, handling inquiries about the Library's programs and services and generating publicity for them. The Educational Liaison Office supervises the thousands of schoolchildren and other groups who visit the Library every year. Many of these visitors come expressly to see the Library's special exhibitions, which are organized and mounted by another division within National Programs, the Exhibits Office. The Publishing Office coordinates the production and printing of the various books and pamphlets the Library offers for free and for sale to the public. The Children's Literature Center is responsible for selecting the Library's materials pertaining to children's literature and administering its reading programs.

The American Folklife Center was created by law in 1976 to preserve and promote American culture. It carries out this congressional directive by

A group of blind people (top) gather for a reading in the Jefferson building in 1902. Today the National Library Service for the Blind and Physically Handicapped offers a variety of services for the visually and physically impaired, including the talking books program and the use of Kurzweil machines (bottom), which convert the printed word into spoken sound.

sponsoring and encouraging research, documentation, publications, and exhibitions. It also houses the Archive of Folk Culture (formerly the Archive of American Folk Song), which has gathered an extensive collection of recordings of songs, instrumental music, and spoken narratives since its founding in 1928. The Archive maintains the Center's reading room and its significant holdings of research and reference materials.

The Library's programs for the visually and physically impaired, which are administered by the National Library Service for the Blind and Physically Handicapped, have expanded greatly since 1897, the year Librarian John Young initiated public readings in a special pavilion at the new Library. Today the Library supports a wide network of services for the blind and the disabled, notably through its highly successful talking books program, in which books are recorded on phonograph records or cassette tapes and are then made available to the disabled. Other programs include the production of books and periodicals in braille and the use of Kurzweil machines, which transfer the printed word into spoken sound. In 1987 these programs reached more than 700,000 people, at a cost of $36 million.

The Law Library

The Law Library is the oldest separate department within the Library of Congress, having been created by law in 1832. In the same legislation Congress placed the Law Library under the regulation of the justices of the Supreme Court. During the period when the Court sat in the Capitol, the Law Library was situated in a room adjacent to the Court's chamber on the ground level. In 1897 it was moved to the new Library building with the Library's other collections. Today the reading room and collections of the Law Library are housed in the Madison Building.

The Law Library's collections form the largest holding of legal materials in the world. These include some 2.5 million volumes, periodicals, and offprints (separately printed copies of original documents). British and American law holdings, which make up roughly one-third of the total inventory, contain the Library's first law collection that was assembled in the Capitol (and which escaped the fire of 1851). About two-thirds of the Law Library's holdings pertain to the laws and legal history of ancient and foreign nations. These range from rare volumes, such as an illuminated manuscript of medieval Norman laws (in Latin), to recent legislation of countries throughout the world.

The Law Library, directed by the law librarian, is organized into five divisions: American-British Law, Hispanic (including Spanish and Portuguese)

Talking Books

In 1877, when Thomas Edison applied for a patent for his tinfoil phonograph, he listed "phonograph books, which will speak to blind people without effort on their part," as one of the potential uses of his invention. Some 50 years later, that dream became a reality.

The Library of Congress began providing embossed (braille) books to blind adults in 1931, but these could not serve the needs of the majority of blind Americans who did not have sufficient fingertip sensitivity to read braille. And so, in 1934, the Library began a program to provide books on records. By 1935, 25 talking books—including the Bible, the Constitution, and several plays by Shakespeare—were available on disc.

These heavy, brittle shellac discs were played at 78 revolutions per minute (RPM) and had an average playing time of only 3 to 5 minutes per side. That meant that a single book took up many discs. The Library then began an ambitious program of technical studies to improve the discs and playback equipment. They focused on narrowing the grooves and slowing playback speed to get more text on each side of a record. In 1927, the Library, in cooperation with the American Foundation for the Blind, acquired rights to a $33\frac{1}{3}$ RPM record with narrower, more closely spaced grooves that could contain 15,000 words on a side—7 years before the long-playing record would be available commercially. The new records were made of a lighter-weight Vinylite compound that could withstand repeated playing and mailing. By June 1937, the program had distributed 145 books, including *Gone with the Wind* on 80 records. Patrons used special phonographs distributed by the Library because standard machines played only 78 RPM.

After World War II, the urgent need for reading materials for blinded veterans spurred new technical developments. By 1963, all discs were produced at $16\frac{2}{3}$ RPM and by 1973 at $8\frac{1}{3}$ RPM. The late 1960s saw the introduction of flexible discs for magazines, which were economical both to produce and to mail. In 1959, the Library began distributing talking books on open-reel magnetic tape. Taped books can be produced by volunteers on their own equipment, which is a particular advantage for special interest items not suitable for mass production. It can be difficult, however, for blind readers to thread reel-to-reel tapes. And so in 1968, the Library began testing tape cassettes. In 1974, it began duplicating books on 2-track cassettes at $\frac{15}{16}$ inches per second (IPS) rather than the commercial speed of $1\frac{7}{8}$ IPS—which fit more material on a single tape. In 1977, the library switched to four-track format. Now a single cassette can provide up to 6 hours of playing time, covering about 200 pages of text. The Library produced its last rigid disc in 1987 and now makes cassettes exclusively.

The program's active research continues as it explores the possibilities of digital recording and the compact disc. But whatever the state of the recording art, the Library of Congress will continue to provide recorded books free of charge to any blind or physically handicapped citizen of the United States who needs them.

Law, European (including Soviet) Law, Far Eastern Law, and Near Eastern and African Law. The area specialists that work in these divisions must be competent in the law and, if they work in the non-English-speaking divisions, in foreign languages as well. They deal with a wide range of often complex inquiries from the public and the government, for example, a foreign attorney's question concerning American corporate law. In addition they handle the bulk of congressional inquiries pertaining to foreign laws—for instance, responding to a representative's request for information about recent legal developments in the People's Republic of China.

The Copyright Office

Since the passage of the copyright law of 1870, which placed all copyright matters under the librarian of Congress and set specific penalties for failure to comply with its provisions, the copyright requirement has been an important source of acquisitions for the Library of Congress. By 1897 the number of people seeking copyrights had grown to such a volume that Congress provided for a separate Copyright Department within the Library (headed by a register

A 1924 application for copyright registration. Congress transferred the Copyright Office from the Patent Office to the Library of Congress in 1870. To gain copyright protection for a creative work, an artist or writer must register his or her work with the Copyright Office, submit copies of the work, and pay a small fee.

71

of copyrights). In the years since then the Copyright Department (later renamed the Copyright Office) has accumulated additional responsibilities. Today, for example, it advises Congress on legislation related to copyright questions, including matters pertaining to new information and communications technologies.

The copyright offers protection to a wide variety of creative works including books, periodicals, manuscript literary compositions, works of art, maps, motion pictures, computer programs, dance choreographies, and other creative productions. Any writer, composer of music, or artist wishing to gain copyright protection for a work must register it with the Copyright Office, submit a copy— or in the case of published works, two copies—of the work and pay a fee of $10. The Copyright Office reviews the paperwork, registers those items that meet the requirements of current legislation, and issues a certificate of copyright. It then offers all deposits to the Library. The Library, however, is not required to accept all of these deposits, which in 1986 amounted to 560,212 works. Contrary to popular belief, it does not keep a copy of every book printed in the United States. The Library tends to keep about two-thirds of the number of copyright deposits—retaining most hardcover books but few paperbacks; all published music, prints, and photographs; and most of the maps that are submitted. Motion pictures, which arrive in large reels and thus present unusual storage problems, are treated differently—they are returned to the applicants after registration, with the provision that the Library can recall copies of those it determines are significant. All materials not kept by the Library are returned to the Copyright Office located in the Madison Building and then stored.

The Congressional Research Service

In 1970, faced with what it regarded to be encroachments by the executive branch and with the increasingly complex social and economic demands of the late 20th century, Congress passed the sweeping Legislative Reorganization Act. Under this legislation, the Congressional Research Service (CRS) was established as an independent department within the Library of Congress, replacing the Legislative Reference Service, which had been created in 1915 to aid Congress in research for its legislation.

The CRS is the reference and research arm of Congress. It does not take sides nor make policy recommendations in presenting information about specific issues to members of Congress. Nor does it draft legislation or write speeches for members (although the Legislative Reference Service once did so). It strives to inform members of Congress of all sides of an issue and to point out the implications of each course of action that Congress considers. When hearings are planned, the CRS assists congressional committees in the selection of expert witnesses who are authorities on subjects under investigation.

In 1912, when Congress was considering the formation of the Legislative Reference Service, Librarian Putnam reported that the Library received on average three or four inquiries per day from members seeking information. In the month of February 1988, by comparison, it received 2,513 inquiries each day from members of Congress. Today the Congressional Research Service responds to more than 400,000 inquiries annually on every conceivable subject of public interest.

Because the business that comes before Congress is wide ranging, the CRS employs a staff of 800, including some 550 specialists with areas of expertise ranging from oceanography to Soviet economics. They are organized within seven subject-area divisions: American Law, Economics, Education and Public Welfare, Environment and Natural Resources Policy, Foreign Affairs and National Defense, Government, and Science Policy Research. To ensure that the CRS gains a full understanding of all the problems and options that pertain to the complex issues it treats, the reports and briefings prepared by specialists in each of these divisions are reviewed by their colleagues in other divisions.

The CRS provides information to Congress in various formats—in traditional printed reports and publications, on microfiche (sheets of microfilm), and increasingly by means of on-line data bases that can be viewed on a computer screen and updated almost instantly. Computer terminals located in congressional offices allow staff members to gain immediate access to several data bases that the CRS maintains as well as to digests of information such as the CRS's *Digest of Public General Bills*, which tracks the progress of each bill introduced into the House and the Senate. The CRS relies primarily upon the collections of the Library of Congress to gather information, but it also draws on research prepared or provided by lobbyists, university research centers, and federal agencies. When a new issue gains public attention, the CRS quickly prepares an overview called an issue brief. This report presents the issue in context, offers analysis of possible solutions to problems, and provides bibliographical references for further investigation. During the Iran hostage crisis of 1980, for example, the CRS updated its issue brief three or four times each day as new information concerning the crisis was received. After an issue

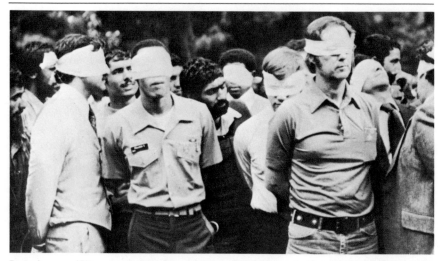

Iranian militants take Americans hostage at the U.S. embassy in Tehran in 1980. During each day of the hostage crisis, the Congressional Research Service updated its analysis, published in an issue brief, as new information about the crisis was received.

brief is released, more substantial and in-depth analysis of the issue is prepared by area specialists, and this information is published in what is called a CRS report. The Congressional Reference Division of the CRS, which is staffed by professional librarians, then makes up an "infopack" on the issue, which includes the CRS report, selections from pertinent documents, a sampling of papers prepared by special interest groups, and a bibliography of sources on the topic.

Members of Congress also rely on the Congressional Research Service to make their staffs more effective and efficient. The CRS provides a program of orientation and training for new congressional staff members and offers advanced sessions for more experienced staff members to update them on new developments that affect their jobs. It also sponsors regular programs on public issues to allow congressional staff members to hear and respond to proponents of legislation and representatives of various interest groups.

Processing Services

The Processing Services divisions, which together form the largest of the six main administrative departments of the Library, are responsible for acquiring, selecting, and controlling the Library's vast collections. The work of purchasing books and printed materials, arranging for exchanges with other libraries, processing gifts, and cataloging the acquisitions is seldom visible to the public. It is nevertheless vital to the operation of the Library of Congress and is essential to the entire legislative branch, for without precise information about the nature and the extent of the Library's holdings, the collections are of limited value. Seventeen of the Library's 85 divisions are engaged in various aspects of the important work of acquiring and processing the collections.

The Library receives between 9 and 10 million new items a year from a variety of sources, although in fiscal year 1987 only 1.2 million of the items received were retained or acquired for its permanent collections. The process of selecting what to keep and what to discard conforms to a carefully considered acquisitions policy and to priorities dictated by the Library's areas of responsibility and expertise. The Library's budget also influences what is retained. Some items, such as books in braille and tape cassettes, which are loaned to the physically handicapped, are used in programs and services provided by the Library but do not become part of the permanent collections.

Acquisitions librarians refer to four categories or standards to make what are frequently difficult decisions about which items the Library should acquire or retain: "comprehensive," meaning that anything available on a given topic is to be acquired; "research," under which significant works on a particular subject are to be acquired; "reference," specifying only the most important or representative works; and "minimal." Many categories and subjects are in fact excluded, such as primary school textbooks, books that are published privately for individuals, medical treatises (which are sent to the National Library of Medicine at the National Institutes of Health in Bethesda, Maryland), and agricultural studies (which are sent to the National Agricultural Library of the Department of Agriculture in Beltsville, Maryland).

The new materials the Library regularly receives come from several sources. The Copyright Office offers all of its receipts to the Library; roughly two-thirds of these are retained, but this usually represents only about 5 percent of the total number of items the Library receives each year. Copies of frequently used titles, needed for the general collections and the Congressional Research Service's reference collection, are purchased directly. Government documents or publications account for more than one-third of the annual incoming flow of receipts. The Library is assisted by federal regulations in meeting its responsibility to secure one or more copies of every significant publication of the federal government, but it often has difficulty obtaining publications issued by state governments, which it acquires selectively for historical as well as Congress's legislative purposes. Copies of significant publications issued by foreign governments (such as laws and legislative reports) are acquired by means of a variety of exchange agreements and programs. Exchange programs as well as direct purchases also bring in foreign books, serials, and periodicals. Finally, the Library benefits each year from the receipt of private gifts, notably of personal papers and other manuscripts.

The work of processing the acquisitions—of identifying and gaining control over the new materials—encompasses (1) describing the physical dimensions and attributes of each book, phonograph record, film reel, periodical, or other incoming item; (2) identifying the item's author or source; (3) classifying the item by the Library of Congress system; and (4) preparing the record or main entry for each title. This work is seldom simple or straightforward. Two-thirds of the materials the Library receives, for example, are in foreign languages, and some 470 foreign languages are represented in the Library's collections. The task of subject cataloging, of deciding the classification and subject heading of each separate item, is often quite complicated—and, if it is to be effective, must anticipate the expectations of users.

Today, the once extremely time-consuming and labor-intensive tasks of gaining control over the Library's collections are more manageable and refined because of the increasingly sophisticated techniques made possible by modern data and information processing. The MARC (MAchine-Readable Cataloging) Editorial Division enters new titles into the Library's computer and then supplies the information to libraries across the country by way of a tape reel or by optical disk, usually on a weekly basis. Two separate divisions within Processing Services are devoted entirely to Automation Planning and Network Development.

Research Services

Research Services is composed of some 21 divisions and units that deal directly with the public in a variety of ways. These units are charged with the care, maintenance, and preservation of the collections, with providing the reference services that assist the public in using them, and with the planning for their improvement and development. The skilled reference librarians and support personnel who staff the various divisions within the department have the most direct contact with the public. They handle the overwhelming majority of inquiries received by the Library from noncongressional sources, which in 1987 amounted to almost 1.9 million requests, and they assist readers and researchers in defining their inquiries or investigations and direct them to the best bibliographical sources or finding aids for their subjects.

The Research Services department embraces the General Reading Rooms Division, which staffs the general reading rooms and is also responsible for the microform collections; the Collections Management Division, which oversees the shelving, retrieval, and inventory of the general (but not the special) collections; the Loan Division, which deals with loans to members of Congress and to the libraries of federal agencies, and also makes loans to other libraries; the Science and Technology Division, which assists the public with technical information and has responsibility for the Science Reading Room; and the Serial and Government Publications Division, which also maintains the Newspaper and Current Periodical Reading Room, the most frequently used specialty reading room in the Library.

Area Studies, a subdepartment of Research Services, is currently composed of four divisions devoted to foreign language collections. These are grouped by culture and geographic region and are divided into the European Division (including the Soviet Union but not Spain and Portugal); the Hispanic Division, comprising Spanish- and Portuguese-speaking countries; the Asian Division, with Chinese and Korean, Japanese, and Southern Asian sections; and the African and Middle East Division. These four divisions employ specialists with foreign language skills who perform bibliographic services related to their subject areas and assist researchers in public reading rooms. The Asian Division contains the oldest books and manuscript items held by the Library.

The Special Collections subdepartment within Research Services is composed of six divisions that supervise many of the Library's most treasured possessions. They are the Manuscript Division; the Rare Book and Special Collections Division; the Geography and Map Division; the Prints and Photographs Division; the Music Division; and the Motion Picture, Broadcasting and Recorded Sound Division. These divisions maintain their own reading rooms and supervise their valuable collections, which, owing to the need for climate control and security, as well as convenience, are housed in special stack areas.

The Library is particularly rich in its more than 10,000 manuscript (derived from the Latin, for "handwritten") collections, maintained by the Manuscript Division. Although the division has gained many important acquisitions from overseas sources, notably the Sigmund Freud Archives, its collections are dominated by the personal papers (letters, diaries, and other original writings) of prominent Americans. The most important of these is the Presidential Papers Series, represented by collections of most American presidents from George Washington to Calvin Coolidge. Also notable are the division's

The Dayton C. Miller Flute Collection

It is well known that the Library of Congress contains more than just books, but few people know that it contains the largest single collection of flutes in the world. The Dayton C. Miller Flute Collection, like many of the Library's treasures, began as a private collection. Its creator, Dayton C. Miller, was a professor of physics at the Case Institute of Science in Cleveland, Ohio, who specialized in acoustic research.

Miller began playing the flute as a child. The son of a hardware store owner in rural Ohio, he also enjoyed working with his hands (he later made several of his own flutes). These interests, combined with his scientific bent, culminated in a lifelong obsession with all things relating to the flute. Over the course of about 50 years, he amassed what is thought to be the largest collection in the world relating to a single musical instrument. In addition to some 1,600 flutes and related instruments, it includes 3,000 books on the history of the flute, about 10,000 pieces of music, 400 prints, 70 statuettes of flute players, 1,000 photographs of flutes and flutists, and uncounted numbers of manufacturers' catalogs and other ephemera (miscellaneous printed materials such as concert programs and newspaper clippings).

When Miller retired in 1940, he intended to transfer his collection to the Library and move to Washington to become its curator. Unfortunately, Miller died in February 1941, before he could make the move, but the collection was bequeathed to the Library under the terms of his will.

The collection is an invaluable tool for organologists—scholars who study the history of musical instruments—and for more general musical historians, who derive much of their information about musical styles and performance from old instruments. The collection effectively traces the history of the flute from

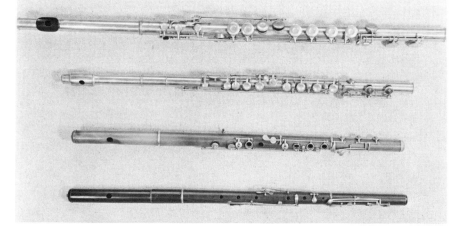

Four flutes by Theobald Boehm show (from bottom to top) the evolution of his fingering system and the switch from wood to silver.

prehistoric times—the earliest specimen is a Chinese egg-shaped instrument from approximately 1100 B.C.—to the modern age—the newest is an experimental silver flute made by a commercial manufacturer in Elkhart, Indiana, in the 1970s. (There have been several additions to the collection since it arrived at the Library.)

The flutes also run the gamut geographically, hailing from such diverse areas as Egypt, Japan, Greece, Sudan, Uganda, and the Philippines as well as Western Europe and the United States. Included are 93 American Indian instruments representing some 32 known tribes; 25 are from as-yet-unidentified tribes. The Indian flutes include a number of curiosities, such as an Osage whistle with a human scalp attached. Over the centuries the flute advanced from a simple vessel, or tube, to become a complicated machine. In the 17th century, it began to acquire primitive keys until it reached its more or less standard form—the 8-key flute—in the early 19th century. The Miller Collection includes literally hundreds of these instruments, representing every significant European flute maker.

Then, in 1832, a German goldsmith and flutist named Theobald Boehm invented the prototype of the modern flute—the first flute whose holes were placed according to acoustical principles rather than where the fingers happened to fall on the tube. The Miller Collection contains 42 instruments from Boehm's own shop, which trace the development of his new fingering system and his switch from wood to silver tubes.

Simultaneous with Boehm's work, however, other European and American flute makers continued to modify the "old system" 8-key flute, sometimes making monstrosities with as many as 18 overlapping and conflicting keys. They also experimented with different materials—not just wood or silver or gold but also ivory, glass, Plexiglas, silver-plated brass, ebonite (a synthetic rubber), and Bakelite (an early form of plastic that was also used for the dance floors in Fred Astaire's movies). There are also walking stick flutes—walking sticks that can actually be played. The Miller Collection contains a broad selection of all these oddities; indeed, one of Miller's flute-maker friends once promised him that he would "be on the lookout for you from now on regarding freaks or experiments." In addition to instruments with true musical significance, the Miller Collection contains a number of flutes with interesting historical associations. One was specially made for the 1876 premiere performance of Verdi's opera *Aida*. Others were played in John Philip Sousa's U.S. Marine Band and in Buffalo Bill's Wild West Show. Perhaps the most beautiful instrument is the one that belonged to King Frederick the Great of Prussia and is stored in an exquisite hand-painted porcelain case. Another historic instrument is the four-key glass flute given by the Marquis de Lafayette to U.S. president James Madison.

Today, the Miller Collection has its own full-time professional curator and is housed in an atmospherically controlled room in the Music Division's new home in the Madison Building. Although not all of the flutes are in playing condition, some are used in concerts in the Library's Coolidge Auditorium, and all are accessible to scholars.

The Rare Book and Special Collections Division maintains its own reading room, located in the Thomas Jefferson Building. The division also has its own climate-controlled stack areas for its more than 300,000 volumes, pamphlets, and other items—judged to be rare for their value to scholarly research rather than for their age.

extensive holdings of papers of prominent American politicians, statesmen, jurists, and military leaders (such as Henry Clay, Henry Kissinger, Felix Frankfurter, and John J. Pershing) and its collections of papers of important social and cultural figures (such as Elizabeth Cady Stanton, Samuel F. B. Morse, Walt Whitman, and Booker T. Washington). The Manuscript Division holds some 900 collections of papers of members of Congress, but it does not accept the official records of agencies of the federal government, which are usually transferred to the National Archives and Records Administration. The Manuscript Division also houses the photocopies of materials in foreign libraries and archives that have been gathered since 1905 by the Library's Foreign Copying Program.

The Rare Book and Special Collections Division holds more than 300,000 volumes, pamphlets, and other items. In general these are judged to be rare and special because of their value to scholarship and research rather than their age, but the Library has begun to assemble all pre-1800 publications for special care and treatment. The division's holdings embrace a variety of subjects and include volumes from libraries of Presidents Thomas Jefferson and Woodrow Wilson, the Vollbehr collection of early printed books, the Lessing J. Rosenwald collection of illustrated books (containing, notably, works of the English artist and poet William Blake), the personal library of the magician and spiritualist Harry Houdini, early Russian imprints, and rare American children's books.

The Library's Geography and Map Division houses the largest and most comprehensive collection of cartographic materials in the world. There are almost 4 million items—some 3.9 million maps and charts of all kinds and sizes, 48,000 atlases, 2,000 three-dimensional cartographic models, and 8,000 reference books. Among those of greatest historical value are 15th- and 16th-century charts used by Spanish and Portuguese explorers, a 1639 map of Manhattan Island, original maps used by troops in the French and Indian War and the American Revolution, and the earliest map of the national capital, Washington, D.C.

The Prints and Photographs Division contains a vast archive of more than 10 million images—photographs and photographic negatives, drawings and cartoons, fine art prints, views in various media, posters, and graphics. The collections form an invaluable visual record, particularly of 19th- and 20th-century America, and are frequently consulted by writers, editors, and

The Library of Congress holds a preeminent collection of Bibles in the Rare Book and Special Collections Division.

81

publishers seeking illustrations for books, magazines, and television programs. The Prints and Photographs Division also holds the Library's collection of architectural drawings, among which can be found original designs for the U.S. Capitol, works of the early American architect Benjamin Henry Latrobe, and surveys of documents pertaining to the nation's architectural heritage, such as the records of the Historical American Buildings Survey (HABS).

The performing arts are the focus of interest for two of the special collections divisions. The Music Division maintains the Library's rare musical instruments and holdings of more than 4 million pieces of music and related papers, some 300,000 books and pamphlets, and about 350,000 sound recordings. The division also produces the chamber music concerts of the Library of Congress, which are held throughout the year in the Grace Sprague Coolidge Auditorium and broadcast live over radio stations nationwide. The Motion Picture, Broadcasting and Recorded Sound Division holds a remarkable collection of the earliest films and recordings (dating from an 1890 wax cylinder recording of an American Indian chant and the 1894 moving picture *Edison Kinetoscopic Record of a Sneeze*), which have been acquired primarily through copyright provisions and donations from collectors. The collection has been

Library specialists in the Geography and Map Division gather around a cartographic model of the Soviet Union, which was created by Leonard Abrams (third from left) and donated to the collection in 1987. The Library contains the world's largest collection of cartographic materials.

Librarian Boorstin (second from right) accompanies some officials from a Washington-based foundation in a tour of the Prints and Photographs Division. The division, located in the James Madison Building, houses more than 10 million photographic images, architectural drawings, and posters.

improved, preserved and restored, and increased over the years as a consequence of cooperative agreements with organizations such as the Academy of Motion Picture Arts and Sciences and the American Film Institute (AFI). Public screenings of films held by the division are presented regularly in the Library's Mary Pickford Theater. The division also contains the American Television and Radio Archives, established in 1978.

The Performing Arts Library, another recently established unit of the Research Services Department, is housed in the John F. Kennedy Center for the Performing Arts. It currently holds a reference collection of more than 5,000 books and periodicals as well as a variety of audiovisual research materials—which is supplemented by the general collections and the holdings of the other special collections division of the Research Services Department. The goal of the Performing Arts Library is to enrich the performing arts by providing reference and research support to performers, designers, writers, and others active in the creation of musical, dance, and theatrical productions.

A computer terminal in the Library's Main Reading Room. Computer technology has greatly improved the Library's storage capabilities and offers new opportunities in processing materials and retrieving information.

FIVE

The Library of Congress in the Information Age

The information age is a useful term to characterize the cumulative social, economic, and cultural changes that have resulted from the technological revolution of the late 20th century. Advances in the technology of microdevices such as the microchip and their applications to mainframe, mini- and personal computers; television and audiovisual technologies; telecommunications; and medical and technical diagnostics are all transforming the American workplace and substantially altering almost every aspect of everyday life.

The rapid computation and communication of data have been welcomed in the business world because they provide information about the marketplace that in turn allows companies to use their resources more effectively. Data stored and processed by the memory capacity of the microchip takes much of the guesswork out of decisions that affect a company's resources of time and money. The efficiencies afforded by these new technologies are by no means limited to the business world, however. They have become essential to the strategic defense of the United States, as well as to the fields of government, education, and medicine. In the medical health field, for example, recent advances in biotechnology (aided by computer technologies) now permit technicians to precisely diagnose many diseases—and in some instances even the likelihood of disease—in patients. The genetic probe, a new technology, has even begun to replace such traditional methods as fingerprinting in the identification of criminals.

Computer and communications technologies have also had significant effects on human behavior and social patterns. Speeding up the flow of information has in effect sped up the pace of life. The realm of the unknown has diminished. News seems to happen more quickly, the public wants answers to its questions within minutes rather than days, patients expect to have precise diagnoses of their conditions almost instantly.

All of these changes have profound implications for the greatest information source in the world, the Library of Congress. The computer technologies have proved applicable to the Library's business of processing and servicing its collections, although the Library has had to develop its own high-tech expertise to adapt these technologies to its own special needs. Still, the assembling, storage, and transportation of data does not automatically add up to knowledge—and fostering knowledge remains at the heart of the Library's national mission. The information age, for all its promise, has brought uncertainties and problems that are no less challenging to the Library of Congress today than were those that confronted Ainsworth Spofford and Herbert Putnam.

The Computer

The Library of Congress began to explore the feasibility of introducing automation to its operations in the late 1950s and 1960s. New dilemmas posed by chronic problems, such as inadequate space for work and storage and a growing backlog in cataloging acquisitions, led Librarian Mumford to seek the advice of outside consultants on the subject. Based largely on a 1963 report that enthusiastically identified the benefits to be gained from automation, the Library took an important step in that direction by assembling a team of experts, from within and outside the Library, to devise a method for converting the printed catalog card to an equivalent format that would be "machine readable." This pilot work led to the development and implementation in early 1966 of the MARC (MAchine-Readable Cataloging) format, which, with refinements, continues in place today.

The success of the MARC project inevitably led to high expectations for computer technologies, particularly in dealing with the Library's cataloging backlogs. Computer systems designed for the Library by outside consultants and contractors did not prove adequate, however, as they did not accommodate

Today the Library of Congress relies on computer systems to catalog its growing collection. The old card catalog, containing more than 20 million printed cards, remains in use; however, the last card was added to the catalog in 1980.

the special characteristics of its vast holdings or anticipate the complex nature of the many different types of requests for information the Library regularly receives. Early projections for computer applications also underestimated the memory capacity that would be required to hold the enormous quantities of information that would have to be entered in order for the computer system to work as a catalog. (The memory capacity of a large computer at that time was about that of a high-quality personal computer today.) By the late 1960s it became feasible for the Library to develop its own capabilities for designing and implementing systems of automation. Today its Automated Systems Office employs some 300 computer specialists and technicians, most of whom are required merely to maintain the systems currently in use.

The Library's current automation systems were developed to accomplish specific tasks and their integration into a single unified system will take time to perfect. Still, the two principal systems used most frequently today, MUMS (Multiple-Use-MARC System) and SCORPIO (Subject-Content-Oriented-Retriever-for-Processing-Information-On-line), permit readers to retrieve a

The Automated Systems Office employs more than 300 computer spe-cialists and technicians who develop and maintain all of the Library's computer systems.

wealth of information about a given subject within minutes. From more than 2,000 terminals across Capitol Hill, the reader or researcher can use simple commands to extract far more specific information about authors and subjects than can be gained (employing the same time and resources) from the old card catalog. The entire computerized catalog of books published in English and Western languages since 1969, for example, can be searched by author, title, or subject. Special use files have been designed for the Copyright Office, the Congressional Research Service, and the Library's internal purposes—these are updated daily or on-line as new information is entered into a file and are in most cases not available to the public.

An Institution in Transition

The Library of Congress formally entered a new era of automation on January 1, 1981. On December 31, 1980, the last printed card was added to the Library's card catalog. Since then the Library has relied solely on its computer systems as the "catalog" to its post-1980 collections.

The Library of Congress card catalog—composed of more than 20 million printed cards in more than 25,000 small file drawers—is still in service and useful for many purposes, although it increasingly has the appearance of a museum object. It will appear even more so with each passing year, for at present more than one-half of the requests made by readers are for books published within the last five years. The pre-1980 card catalog is gradually being entered into the Library's computer by means of a PREM (PRE-MARC) system, although it will take several years to complete this difficult process.

Today there are banks of computer terminals in the principal reading rooms of the Library of Congress and reference librarians on duty to assist researchers in using several retrieval programs to find titles on their subjects. Close by are optical disk readers that one day may be used to call up select titles in the Library's holdings. Although the information stored and available for display is for the most part still kept on Capitol Hill, for the use of Congress and the Library's patrons, it is likely, given the dynamics of the information age, that the Library's catalog and other computer-generated finding aids will be more widely accessible in the future.

The new technologies are having and will continue to have a profound effect on the ways in which the public uses the Library. Readers are increasingly becoming users of computer data bases and viewers of photographic images of books and documents. Advances in photoduplication technology have for some time contributed to this trend, while the physical handling they encourage has placed books and other publications at greater risk. More important, the rate at which the collections are being destroyed by the irreversible process of chemical disintegration has forced the Library to devote much of its attention and resources to preservation and to image- and word-storage technologies.

New capabilities and services such as these are as vital as they are useful to the nation's research effort in the late 20th century. In this age of rapid discoveries in strategic fields such as biotechnology, computer technologies, and the physics of high-tech materials, the answers to pressing questions are often out of date by the time they appear in book or printed report form. The possibility of being able to gather centralized bibliographical information from a computer terminal without traveling to Washington revives both the promise for scholarship envisioned by Herbert Putnam when he inaugurated the printed card service in 1901 and the expectations that lay behind the formation of the National Union Catalog in 1927.

If computer technology offers new opportunities both in processing new materials and in retrieving information, the advent of the information age has nevertheless produced a new set of problems for the Library of Congress. There are new problems, for example, in the area of acquisitions. The increasing capabilities and reliability of information storage technologies have made hard-copy publications less necessary. This is particularly noticeable in the case of state government reports, which are increasingly prepared and stored on digital and image-processing media and are thus more difficult to collect. Furthermore, the cutting edge of fast-changing computer technologies is in the hands of innovators capable of responding to small openings of opportunity presented by the need for increased efficiency and economy. New services developed by private enterprise frequently compete with and replace services offered by the Library of Congress and other government agencies. Although this competition may reduce federal revenues in the short term, and even displace workers, it is productive and beneficial in the long term if the federal government is relieved of costly operations that are not directly related to its statutory responsibilities.

In the near future the promise of greater benefits to be gained by expanding and extending the Library's computer services may be offset to an extent by questions relating to security and institutional and jurisdictional prerogatives. Congress has not yet sanctioned the creation of a national library network, the need for which is not universally acknowledged. Nevertheless, the Library's MARC data base is now accessible through more than 360 federal libraries and information centers and also, as a consequence of cooperative cataloging agreements, through several university libraries and other library networks. The records from a number of institutions have already been added to the Library's master files through the Linked Systems Project (LSP). For example, in the late 1980s, Indiana University, Yale University, Princeton University, and the University of Michigan have contributed records to the files maintained at the Library of Congress via the LSP but through the OCLC system and the Research Libraries Information Network (RLIN). In time, the pressure to eliminate duplication of effort should overcome institutional and organizational resistance to the formation of a nationwide library network based at the Library of Congress.

Paper Crisis

As the Library continues to adjust to the demands of the information age, it must at the same time contend with a crisis created in the past. A substantial portion of its collections are rapidly deteriorating because of the high acid content in books printed on paper made from wood pulp. Books published prior to about 1850 were usually printed on paper made from rags or linen, which survive quite well. When rag supplies diminished, however, and the price of rag paper consequently rose, publishers turned to wood pulp as a substitute for paper production, ignoring the chemical time bomb in the new paper: Paper made from wood pulp is brown and contains lignin glue to bind the fibers—it is whitened by adding alum, and the ingredients in lignin and alum combine to form sulfuric acid. Even though paper companies are able to manufacture acid-free paper—which libraries have been urging for years—the publishing industry, with the exception of some fine arts and most university presses, continues to rely on the acidic variety for financial reasons.

Today the Library estimates that the pages and bindings of roughly one-quarter of its 20 million books are so brittle that they cannot be read

A microfilm technician photographs a valuable book. The introduction of microfilming ensured the protection of original works from wear and tear.

A library technician places decaying books in a vacuum chamber where they will be exposed to the gas DEZ. Deacidification processes continue to be explored by the Library, which needs a method that can treat many books at one time—without damaging the books.

without being damaged. Some 77,000 additional volumes become useless each year, and the increased handling of post-1850 books (few of which are classified as rare) for photoduplication purposes accelerates damage to these books. If nothing is done to stop the chemical process, the Library estimates that 97 percent of its holdings will eventually disintegrate.

The Library has recognized the crisis for some time, however, although the magnitude of the problem has only become apparent in recent years. It began attacking the issue of paper disintegration some 25 years ago, when it launched a major effort to microfilm deteriorating volumes, a program that continues today. But this effort has not kept pace with the rate of deterioration, and it has since become clear that microfilm-based media themselves suffer irreversible decomposition. Methods of deacidification, which neutralize the acid content in books and other items, usually by means of a liquid chemical bath, are time-consuming and depend on special handling. They are thus inappropriate for the vast number of books in the general collections.

The Library's preservation experts have been working since 1973 to develop a practical method for deacidifying books. After many trials and setbacks, it now appears that they have developed a chemical process that will effectively neutralize the acid content of most books published since 1850. The secret of this new method is diethyl zinc (DEZ) gas, which is capable of penetrating damaged books in large numbers while they are closed, eliminating the need for special handling of the individual pages. The technology for this project is still in the developmental stage, but a number of books have been treated in a small-scale pilot project being carried out near Houston, Texas. By this method, books are placed in a vacuum chamber and exposed to gaseous DEZ (liquid DEZ is highly flammable when it comes into contact with oxygen) for a period of 50 to 55 hours. Although other mass deacidification processes have been developed, none of these methods meets the Library's need for a process capable of treating large numbers of books simultaneously—without damaging the paper, ink, or binding materials of the volumes. Once the technology of DEZ mass deacidification has been perfected, the Library hopes that batches of between 1,000 to 3,000 books can be treated at one time. Even at that pace, however, it will take some 20 years of round-the-clock exposures (at an estimated cost of $100 million) to treat all of the materials that are disintegrating. Technicians estimate that a book on medium quality wood-pulp paper that was expected to disintegrate in 50 years will now, after DEZ treatment, last between 150 and 250 years. Still, the new process will only arrest the chemical process within the wood-pulp paper; it will not repair existing damage to the books.

The Promise of Optical Disk Technology

Because the process of disintegration cannot be stopped and because of other problems in the Library, including security, storage, and demands for photo-duplication services, the Library has turned to another promising new technology, the optical disk, for a long-range solution. The optical disk is quite similar in format to the videodisc and the compact disc: A laser burns images of original objects into either an analog optical disk, which stores image-based materials such as illustrations, or a digital optical disk, which compresses and stores printed texts. The images thus produced are durable and of high resolution; the disks, which are currently made of industrial glass, are sturdy and easily shelved and serviced.

One thin 12-inch disk is capable of storing between 10,000 and 20,000 pages of text. A recent Library study estimates that each analog optical disk would store 116 volumes of approximately 350 pages and that a "foot of optical disks standing side by side will thus store over 10,000 volumes and eliminate the

A computer specialist inputs data onto an optical disk. Optical disk technology will provide long-range solutions to storage and preservation problems: One thin 12-inch disk is capable of storing from 10,000 to 20,000 pages of text.

94

need for nearly 1,000 feet of shelving." For digital optical disks the estimated number of volumes that can be stored on one disk rises to 3,200.

The Library is understandably enthusiastic about the potential for optical disk technology, which is being tested and implemented under a pilot program. In 1988, it was projected that optical disks would be used to provide service copies of books and other items in the Library's collections so that the originals could be preserved and protected. In 1983, however, the Library predicted that "some disks will reproduce items with sufficient quality to permit the Library to consider discarding the original." This option would presumably make it easier to dispense with many poor-quality unbound publications, copies of later editions of works judged to be of minor significance, and similar materials. The long-range storage, or archival, properties of optical disks, however, are still undergoing scientific study.

The Library has recently begun to employ optical disk technology to produce cataloging and bibliographical materials for sale to other libraries. This new service will allow libraries and institutions to gain the Library's subject authority file, heretofore only available on magnetic tape (requiring the use of a costly mainframe minicomputer), by means of a disk that can be operated by a standard optical disk reader hooked up to a standard IBM personal computer. As the Library's *Information Bulletin* recently observed, "With only a small investment in computer hardware, large and small computers can now access huge information sources conveniently and easily." Through these and other programs still being tested, the Library continues to be a forerunner in the development and use of advanced technology in the area of librarianship.

A stonecarver chisels the name of the 13th librarian of Congress— James H. Billington—into the wall of the Great Hall.

SIX

The Library of Congress and the Twenty-first Century

The anticipation of a new century and, with the year 2000, of a new millennium has already caused many institutions to give unusual attention to plans for the future. Under Librarian James H. Billington, the Library of Congress has already begun a comprehensive review and planning process with the target year 2000 in mind. As a historian of Russian history and culture, Billington places the Library in a new position of importance during a period that may be dramatically changed by improving relations between the United States and the Soviet Union.

At the end of 1987, Billington announced that three advisory groups would meet during 1988 to "consider how we should begin shaping the Library of Congress now, to the job it should be doing for the 21st century." He indicated that one of these groups would be appointed from the Library's national and international constituencies and that a professional management consulting firm would be engaged to make recommendations on administration and management. Recognizing the need for broad participation within the Library, Billington pledged to form a third group from the ranks of the Library staff.

The Management and Planning (MAP) Committee, organized by Billington and comprised of 25 members of the library staff, reviews the Library's activities and recommends future goals and ways to accomplish them.

This committee, which he designated the Library's Management and Planning (MAP) Committee, would consist of 27 mid-level staff members, chosen as individuals rather than as official representatives of the Library's various departments and divisions. The MAP Committee would be charged with reviewing the Library's role in serving Congress, the federal government, American and foreign libraries, and the community of scholars and artists. Based on its findings, the committee would recommend broad goals the Library should pursue and would suggest the means to accomplish them. Billington also called for an examination of means by which the institution could "reach out more broadly" by "sharing its resources and disseminating its wisdom more widely and effectively in ways that raise educational levels." At the same time, however, he asked the committee "to recommend priorities for the allocation of the Library's resources in light of present and foreseeable budget stringencies."

Although Billington has stressed his desire for the planning process to be "open" and "dynamic," the trend toward automation will continue to shape the Library's future to a large extent. The MAP Committee nevertheless has the opportunity to devise ways to adapt the new technologies to the Library's traditional roles and to make the transition to a new era of automation easier for the public as well as the Library's employees.

Continuing Trends

The major factors that will shape the Library's future have already been identified. Because the chemical disintegration of wood-pulp paper cannot at present be arrested, the Library's attention and resources will increasingly be occupied by the need to preserve its collections. The Optical Disk Pilot Program—and the technologies that support it—will steadily expand and likely be adopted throughout the Library. The Library's Mass Deacidification Program to treat deteriorating books will expand and become more efficient, and new technologies will be examined for their promise. In a new century that will be increasingly shaped by the powers of biochemical engineering, it is not unthinkable that a new process to stop the deterioration of wood-pulp papers will eventually be discovered. It is also possible that new processes that reduce the production costs of acid-free paper will be perfected, thereby permitting publishers to print books that will once again be long lasting.

Computer applications will continue to improve and expand, bringing a greater capacity for service to the nation's community of libraries, now numbering more than 100,000. The promise of computer and telecommunica-

A specialist in the Library's conservation laboratory works to preserve an old periodical. The Library continually conducts research to find more efficient methods for the preservation of paper.

tions technologies for the storage and retrieval of bibliographic information, which seemed to herald a new era of librarianship in the early 1960s, is still compelling. Recent advances in superconductivity (the flow of electric current without resistance in certain metals at temperatures near absolute zero), which will in time reduce substantially the amount of energy needed to operate computer and telecommunications equipment, are truly revolutionary and suggest astounding possibilities. Storage technologies for computer systems will continue to improve, and with these advances the Library may no longer need to expand its physical size to store books and other materials.

Congress's need for up-to-date information will grow, and the Library will, as a consequence, expand its role and capabilities as a clearinghouse of data for the use of government. As a result of the increasing complexity of life in the 21st century, the Congressional Research Service will have to expand to keep pace with the research and reference demands of the Congress. The Library can rely on the legislative branch to provide the additional funding that will be necessary to keep it equipped with the latest in information technologies, but if other areas of the Library's budget are neglected, there is the potential for a renewal of the historic conflict over the Library's dual nature.

Social Effects

As the computer age progresses, more and more information services will be available in the workplace and the home through the computer terminal, and these terminals will be located farther and farther away from the central source of information, the mainframe computer. There will likely be less and less need for readers—who are increasingly being referred to as "users"—to come to the Library of Congress. Eventually local and regional libraries will be affected by the same phenomenon. Such changes represent great advances for those with physical impairments, but they promise to reinforce an unsettling trend of the late 20th century—the decline of public, or civic, life.

The Library of Congress has already responded to these troubling trends, which, if not arrested, would diminish its role and influence in American life. It has adopted many of the educational and public relations methods employed by popular public museums and is actively promoting programs that also encourage readers to use the collections of their local libraries. It has formed the Center for the Book to encourage greater interest in reading and a wider knowledge and appreciation of the history of the book and the printed word. The Library has taken an active role in the national effort to reduce and eliminate illiteracy

In 1988 John Y. Cole, director of the Center for the Book (third from left), presents a copy of the Center's poster to six-year-old Taryn Younus, who was a winner of one of the Center's many reading contests that encourage the appreciation of books.

and the lack of will to read, putting forward a national agenda for action in an important report to Congress, *Books for the Nation*, in 1984. Through these efforts the Library hopes to renew itself as a great public center and cultural forum to which, whether for lectures or concerts, exhibitions or films, research or information gathering— or merely out of sheer curiosity—the nation of terminal gazers and screen viewers will be attracted for enjoyment and enrichment.

The Book and the Future

In the not-too-distant future, the reader will be able to scan a terminal or video screen to find a book or periodical, punch in a code number for it, call up a storage disk from a giant jukeboxlike machine, bring the text of the book onto the same screen, and make a photocopy of a given page by pressing a button.

A patron in the Library's Main Reading Room. Despite the increasing use of personal computers by readers, they continue to enjoy handling the original books.

Even if the book is rare, the reader will not need to travel great distances to the library that holds the original book, which will thereby be protected from rough handling and potential damage.

The Library's expanding role as Congress's clearinghouse of information, the benefits of optical disk technology, and the growing problem of paper disintegration nevertheless suggest that the presence of the physical book in the Library of Congress of the 21st century will be somewhat diminished. Public interest in recently published books will surely not lessen. But books more than 50 years old may increasingly become museum objects and require special handling and treatment. Older books will be available for special purposes and for display in exhibits, but they will be less visible. With actual books and periodicals assuming a secondary role to computers and other advanced technologies, the atmosphere of the Library will inevitably be affected.

These changes will not in themselves lessen the influence of the book. Older books, like the books that are identified as rare today, may in fact be more valued for their fragile, antique, and historic qualities. The expansion of alternative formats for storing and reproducing the printed word—with the inevitable growth of public awareness of the crisis presented by paper disintegration—may actually foster a new sensitivity to books among the general public. Still, it seems clear that the video-dominated culture of the 21st century will not gain an appreciation for books and the printed word unless reading skills are taught and reinforced on every educational level.

The Library and Democracy

In the 21st century, the Library of Congress can best serve the cause of democracy and freedom by continuing to serve as both Congress's library and the nation's library. In that way it will remain close to the American people and to the forces that affect their lives. At the same time it will preserve for them the heritage of human civilization and spirit of enlightenment upon which democratic culture depends if it is to survive. Restoration of the Thomas Jefferson Building, and particularly of the magnificent domed Main Reading Room, scheduled to be completed in 1993, will serve to remind the nation of the Library's great traditions and keep the Library mindful of its enormous responsibilities to the future.

The Library of Congress*

MANAGEMENT SERVICES

Affirmative Action Office
Equal Employment Opportunity Complaints Office
Women's Program Office

Automated Systems Office
Central Services Division
Financial Management Office
Library Support Services Office
Personnel and Labor Relations Office
Photoduplication Service
Procurement and Supply Division

CONGRESSIONAL RESEARCH SERVICE

Office of Automated Information Services
Office of Management and Administrative Services
Office of Member and Committee Relations
Office of Policy, Planning, and Review
Office of Research, Analysis, and Multidisciplinary Programs
Office of Senior Specialists
Senior Specialists

American Law Division
Economics Division
Education and Public Welfare Division
Environment and Natural Resources Policy Division
Foreign Affairs and National Defense Division
Government Division
Science Policy Research Division

Office of Assignment, Reference, and Special Services
Congressional Reference Division
Library Services Division

COPYRIGHT OFFICE

Receiving and Processing Division
Cataloging Division
Deposits and Acquisitions Division
Examining Division
Information and Reference Division
Licensing Division

LAW LIBRARY

American-British Law Division
European Law Division
Far Eastern Law Division
Hispanic Law Division
Near Eastern and African Law Division

* This organizational chart was in effect until December 31, 1988.

104

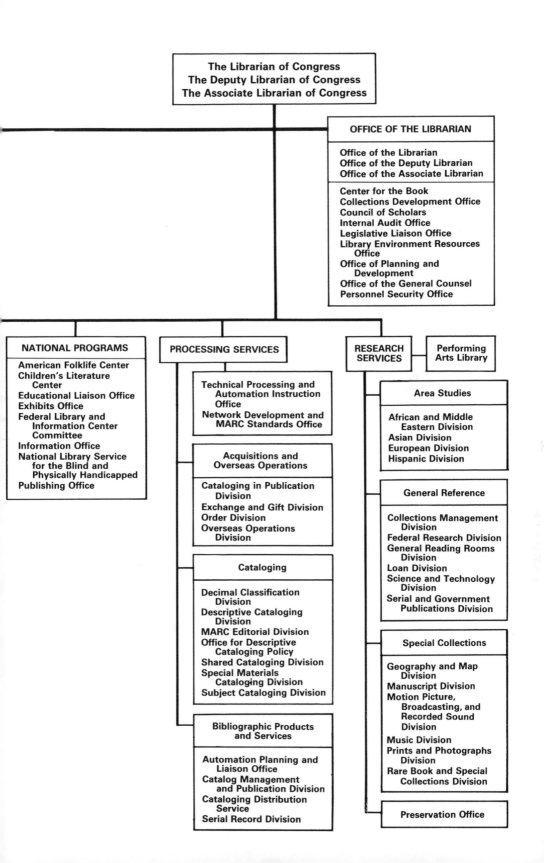

The Librarian of Congress
The Deputy Librarian of Congress
The Associate Librarian of Congress

OFFICE OF THE LIBRARIAN

Office of the Librarian
Office of the Deputy Librarian
Office of the Associate Librarian

Center for the Book
Collections Development Office
Council of Scholars
Internal Audit Office
Legislative Liaison Office
Library Environment Resources
    Office
Office of Planning and
    Development
Office of the General Counsel
Personnel Security Office

NATIONAL PROGRAMS

American Folklife Center
Children's Literature
    Center
Educational Liaison Office
Exhibits Office
Federal Library and
    Information Center
    Committee
Information Office
National Library Service
    for the Blind and
    Physically Handicapped
Publishing Office

PROCESSING SERVICES

Technical Processing and
    Automation Instruction
    Office
Network Development and
    MARC Standards Office

Acquisitions and
Overseas Operations

Cataloging in Publication
    Division
Exchange and Gift Division
Order Division
Overseas Operations
    Division

Cataloging

Decimal Classification
    Division
Descriptive Cataloging
    Division
MARC Editorial Division
Office for Descriptive
    Cataloging Policy
Shared Cataloging Division
Special Materials
    Cataloging Division
Subject Cataloging Division

Bibliographic Products
and Services

Automation Planning and
    Liaison Office
Catalog Management
    and Publication Division
Cataloging Distribution
    Service
Serial Record Division

**RESEARCH
SERVICES**

**Performing
Arts Library**

Area Studies

African and Middle
    Eastern Division
Asian Division
European Division
Hispanic Division

General Reference

Collections Management
    Division
Federal Research Division
General Reading Rooms
    Division
Loan Division
Science and Technology
    Division
Serial and Government
    Publications Division

Special Collections

Geography and Map
    Division
Manuscript Division
Motion Picture,
    Broadcasting, and
    Recorded Sound
    Division
Music Division
Prints and Photographs
    Division
Rare Book and Special
    Collections Division

Preservation Office

Library of Congress
CONCEPT OF OPERATIONS†

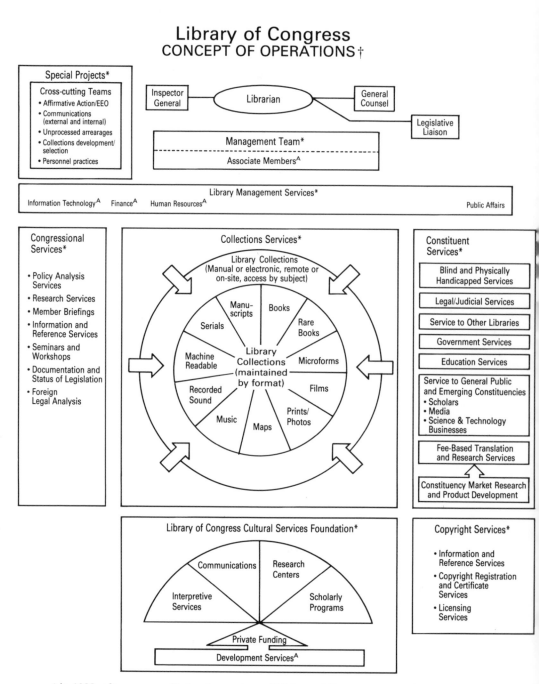

Special Projects*

Cross-cutting Teams
- Affirmative Action/EEO
- Communications (external and internal)
- Unprocessed arrearages
- Collections development/selection
- Personnel practices

Inspector General

Librarian

General Counsel

Legislative Liaison

Management Team*
- -
Associate Members[A]

Library Management Services*

Information Technology[A]   Finance[A]   Human Resources[A]   Public Affairs

Congressional Services*
- Policy Analysis Services
- Research Services
- Member Briefings
- Information and Reference Services
- Seminars and Workshops
- Documentation and Status of Legislation
- Foreign Legal Analysis

Collections Services*

Library Collections (Manual or electronic, remote or on-site, access by subject)

Manuscripts   Books   Serials   Rare Books   Machine Readable   Library Collections (maintained by format)   Microforms   Recorded Sound   Films   Music   Maps   Prints/Photos

Constituent Services*

Blind and Physically Handicapped Services

Legal/Judicial Services

Service to Other Libraries

Government Services

Education Services

Service to General Public and Emerging Constituencies
- Scholars
- Media
- Science & Technology Businesses

Fee-Based Translation and Research Services

Constituency Market Research and Product Development

Library of Congress Cultural Services Foundation*

Communications   Research Centers   Interpretive Services   Scholarly Programs

Private Funding

Development Services[A]

Copyright Services*
- Information and Reference Services
- Copyright Registration and Certificate Services
- Licensing Services

† In 1988, after a year of intensive review of Library of Congress operations, a MAP (Management and Planning) Committee recommended a new organizational concept for the Library. The Library began working under the plan in January 1989.

106

GLOSSARY

Archives   A place in which records or historical documents are preserved.

Athenaeum   A building or room in which books, periodicals, and newspapers are kept for use.

Bibliography   A list of writings or publications on a particular subject, or a list of works of a specific author.

Braille   A system of writing for the blind that uses characters made up of raised dots.

Card catalog   A system used by libraries in which each item is recorded on a card and filed alphabetically according to title, author, and subject.

Congressional Research Service   A branch of the Library that provides Congress with data and information for its legislation.

Copyright   The exclusive legal right to reproduce, publish, and sell a literary, musical, or artistic work.

Deacidification   A process used to neutralize the acid content in books and other items in order to delay their decay.

Dewey Decimal Classification   A system of classifying books and other publications, used by most elementary and secondary school libraries and small public libraries in the United States, in which major categories are designated by a three-digit number and subdivisions are shown by numbers after a decimal point.

MARC (MAchine-Readable Cataloging)   A bibliographic automation program, begun by the Library in 1966, in which participating libraries with computers would receive reels of tape containing bibliographic records and could then use these tapes to print their own catalog cards.

Microfiche   A sheet of microfilm capable of preserving a considerable number of pages of printed matter in reduced form.

SELECTED REFERENCES

Cole, John Y. "For Congress & the Nation." *Quarterly Journal of the Library of Congress* 32 (April 1975): 118–38.

Copyright Law of the United States of America. Circular 92. Washington, DC: U.S. Copyright Office, Library of Congress, September 30, 1987.

Edlund, Paul. "A Monster and a Miracle: The Cataloging Distribution Service of the Library of Congress, 1901–1976." *Quarterly Journal of the Library of Congress* 33 (October 1976): 383–421.

Goodrum, Charles A. *Treasures of the Library of Congress.* New York: Abrams, 1980.

Goodrum, Charles A., and Helen W. Dalrymple. *Guide to the Library of Congress.* Washington, DC: Library of Congress, 1988.

———. *The Library of Congress.* Boulder, CO: Westview Press, 1982.

Hilker, Helen-Anne. *Ten First Street, Southeast: Congress Builds a Library, 1886–1897.* Washington, DC: Library of Congress, 1982.

Johnston, William Dawson. *History of the Library of Congress.* Vol. 1, 1800–1864. Washington, DC: Government Printing Office, 1904.

Mearns, David C. *The Story Up to Now: The Library of Congress, 1800–1946.* Washington, DC: Library of Congress, 1947.

Rensberger, Boyce. "Acid Test: Stalling Self-Destruction in the Stacks." *Washington Post,* August 29, 1988: A13.

Rohrbach, Peter. *Find: Automation at the Library of Congress, The First Twenty-five Years and Beyond.* Washington, DC: Library of Congress, 1985.

Small, Herbert. *The Library of Congress: Its Architecture and Decoration.* New York: Norton, 1982.

U.S. Library of Congress. *Annual Report of the Librarian of Congress.* Washington, DC: Library of Congress, 1866–   .

———. *Librarians of Congress, 1802–1974.* Washington, DC: Library of Congress, 1977.

———. *Quarterly Journal of the Library of Congress.* Washington, DC: Library of Congress, 1943–   .

INDEX

110

Andrew L. Simpson is an editor and a historian of early American culture. He received a B.A. and a Ph.D. in American history and has taught history and social studies on the junior high and secondary school levels and U.S. and Canadian history on the college and graduate school levels.

Arthur M. Schlesinger, jr., served in the White House as special assistant to Presidents Kennedy and Johnson. He is the author of numerous acclaimed works in American history and has twice been awarded the Pulitzer Prize. He taught history at Harvard College for many years and is currently Albert Schweitzer Professor of the Humanities at the City College of New York.